# FROM INTERNMENT TO FULFILLMENT

## HOW TO SHIFT INTO PEACE, PURPOSE AND

## PROSPERITY AGAINST ALL ODDS

By

Neary Heng with David M. Corbin

Published by Freedoms

Copyright © 2015 by Neary Heng

First Printed in 2015 in the United States of America.

ISBN-13: 978-1515371748

ISBN-10: 1515371743

## What people are saying about

## FROM INTERNMENT TO FULFILLMENT

*"Over 10 million readers have learned the Fish! Philosophy on morale. From Internment to Fulfillment reveals Neary's strategy for creating happiness anywhere, anytime."* - **Harry Paul**, Co-Author <u>FISH: A Remarkable Way to Boost Morale and Improve Results.</u>

*"I faced so many obstacles on the way to competing in four Winter Olympic Games. I truly wish I had read Neary Heng's S.B.C.I.A. strategy early on my Olympic journey. Success really does require an element of stubbornness."*—**Ruben Gonzalez,** Olympian, Author, Speaker

*"As an avid reader, I can say without hesitation that this is one of the most inspiring reads because of Neary's courage and tenacity. I'm inspired by how true she remained to her beliefs and values."* - **Phil Wexler**, Hall of Fame Speaker, Author.

*"In my book <u>Stickability</u>, I exposed strategies on staying the course even when things are tough. Neary Heng is the embodiment of those principles. Her strategy is a simple and effective process you can apply today and prepare yourself for the issues of tomorrow."* - **Greg Reid**, Speaker, Filmmaker, Author of *Think and Grow Rich - Three Feet From Gold* and *Stickability*.

*"Making up products for market, inventing them and inventing services has been relatively easy in my 40+year career. I don't see problems, I see challenges. Neary and I are on the same page here. When confronted with challenges, even at a very early age, she rises to the occasion and does so very effectively. You will too after reading this book. Read it now."* - **Ron Klein**, The Grandfather of Possibility, Inventor of the magnetic stripe on credit cards

*"Neary's life so at the example of courage and skills. I'm inspired to apply both. From Internment to Fulfillment is Awesome."* - Speaker **Erik "Mr. Awesome" Swanson**, Best-Selling Author of <u>Secret Habitudes</u>

*"Neary Heng is a natural writer and refreshingly easy to read. Her wisdom to live life by her acronym S.B.C.I.A., is something that I am going to integrate into my life from now on. Her story is a unique example of adversity forging the power to embrace*

life's uncertainties with strength and humor." - **Brian Smith**, UGG Australia Founder, Author and Speaker.

"This is a wonderful book that educates and uplifts with riveting stories on overcoming tough conditions. After reading it... I must, I can, I will!" - **Mitch Axelrod**, Author of *Soul, Role, Goal*

"Even as a young girl, Neary knew that every adversity carried what with it a lesson of opportunity. What an inspiration she is to convert so many obstacles into positive life lessons. Read them and apply them." - **Ed Bogle**, Master Strategist, Author of *Focus Strategy for Success*

"I'm a big proponent of personal responsibility in business and in life. This story is an example of how one does just that." - **Aaron Young**, CEO of Laughlin Associates, Inc.

"Neary's stories are nothing short of miraculous. The lessons she teaches overlap with some of what I discovered in co-founding the Make-A-Wish Foundation. I just wish this book was available way back then!" - **Frank Shankwitz**, Co-Founder of Make-A-Wish Foundation

"Sometimes motivator needs motivation herself... and this book is just that." - **Loral Langemeier**, CEO & Founder of Live Out Loud, Inc., Money Expert, Speaker, Best-selling Author

*"Believe in yourself. When you believe in yourself, there are many possibilities that open up for you. Neary is the prime example."* - **Joseph Sugarman**, Legendary Copywriter and Direct Marketing Pioneer.

## ACKNOWLEDGEMENT OF MY MOM, LANG

Mom, I would like you to know that David and I were working on the final edits for this book last Tuesday. We were looking for quality words to describe you.

Mom, we would like to honor you with accuracy, love, and respect. And so in the process, as we were going through various chapters, we came up with a list of words that we thought were appropriate to describe you and why. It was really interesting to us to do that because although this book is about my life, my experience, of course, none of this would have happened without you, your life, your experience and the qualities that you brought to everything in this book and everything in my life outside of this book. I honor you with some of these words:

> *Resourceful, observant, strategic, sacrificial, amazingly aware, thrifty, creative in everything that you have done, as you're so loyal and attached to your children, your husband, your employer, your sense of responsibility, and above all your amazing courage in all situations.*

These are qualities that someday I hope someone will attach or attribute to me because it means so much to me ... And most of all mother, I honor you; my brother and I, honor you. There are no words that can express our gratitude for what you've done, what you've given, and most important, who you are.

# Contents

## Introduction

I have always been smaller than kids my age, and when I would get picked on, I can recall my Mom's guidance, "David, I want to remind you that most good things in life come in small packages." Gee, thanks, Mom. How's THAT going to help me?

Like a lot of advice from my parents, there was an enormous delay until I "got it." I know you can relate.

The "small packages" observation came to mind many years later when I met Neary Heng, because at under 5 feet tall, weighing not much more than 20 phone books, this little powerhouse blew my mind. After some warming up, she shared stories and life conditions that she endured during her early years in Cambodia when the Khmer Rouge regime was in power, took over the nation and murdered millions of her fellow countrymen, women, and children. And to think, this happened in my lifetime. Her stories had me sitting on edge of my seat, oddly enough sometimes laughing my ass off, and at other times, literally wiping tears from my eyes. I was amazed that someone could go through so much adversity and not only overcome, but survive, despite so many challenges and still emerge to be the epitome of positivity and happiness.

The stories you are about to read are all real or based on true experiences that Neary personally experienced. Some of these stories are reminiscent of fiction stories that are developed into screenplays for the big screen in movie theaters. However, these stories and life lessons are based on real experiences virtually shared from her very rich life.

When Neary asked me to assist her in the development of this book, I interviewed her as I often do when so approached. When she first told me that her mission was to facilitate happiness in these "interesting times," I rolled my eyes in cynical judgment. But, my mom also taught me to be polite and caring, or at least polite and respectful. Happily, we were on the telephone and she didn't see that! I mean, c'mon, "facilitate happiness"?

So I asked her some questions, expecting to get more of the "nicey nice, feel-good rhetoric," but Neary surprised me. Instead, I got stories that showed me that Neary is not only substantive in her approach to dealing with adversity, but also pragmatically organized. What I mean by that is she has created strategies to not only cope and deal with adversity, but to also leverage and benefit from them.

What an honor it's been assisting Neary to clarify the thoughts and recollections around her lessons. And in the process, I benefited beyond imagination from the gentle strength, humor, raw emotion, and wisdom beyond her years revealed in these stories and her tried-and-true, field-tested strategies.

In between our working sessions, I found myself thinking about and applying these strategies and was delighted to find that they are relevant and transferable in my life … and the results came rather quickly. I was impressed.

I'm grateful to Neary for sharing so openly and courageously some of the many unbelievably tough moments in her life.

I'm also grateful to my mom. Why? Because without her wisdom and advice, I could easily have blown Neary off and not seriously learned and benefited from her stories, her life path, her lessons, and her passion for life, love, and giving back.

It's with great courage and love that Neary offers this book to you. I am proud to have the honor of introducing this remarkable woman and her book. The stories are real, and so is Neary's upstanding character, determination, and devout sincerity in bringing them to you.

You will find within its pages the cascade of emotions which, if you are anything like me, will find you involved, motivated, inspired, and driven to apply each and every chapter's lesson. And when you do, you will be in good company, along with many of the people who read this book and offered the powerful testimonials in its first few pages.

Neary Heng is a testament to the fact that good things come in small packages. How cool is it that this "small, under 5' tall package" has motivated BIG motivators and educated BIG educators such as the ones her book's testimonials? I expect that you will add your accolades to theirs after reading her wonderful story. Most important, I fully expect that you will leverage some of these rich lessons to achieve additional peace, purpose, and prosperity in your life.

David M. Corbin

E-mail: david@davidcorbin.com

San Diego, California

**Dear Gentle Reader:**

I've been pretty much a shy, introvert person throughout my whole life. It is awkward for me to get naked in front of you between the covers of this book. You'll read stories in which I exposed myself ... Well, at least my emotions, through the sharing of real life experiences since my earliest recollections.

I'm writing this letter from the comfort of my beautiful home in sunny southern California. I'm safe, comfortable, nurture, healthy, at peace, and happy with freedom.

I always knew that I would be, but I had my doubts as you'll soon learn. However, my doubts were short lived simply because I tapped into a source of hope, energy, faith, always seeking for help and resilience, which is fortified by courage and creativity. I just thought I was a normal little girl. The rudeness and depression which led to nearby killings and servitudes were, I thought, normal.

My desire for peace, freedom, health, happiness, and prosperity will always there and, therefore, I assumed these experiences were testing and strengthening me through the journey of life. And they were.

However, I was old enough to understand only a small percentage of people had experienced these level of challenges and how so many didn't survive.

I had the enormous epiphany that my life experiences were part of the very small percentage of the people. I had no idea that the hand of life that I was dealt was much more challenging than most.

I wish I could say that I remain positive at all times, but the truth is I have my days. I had my darkest difficult days, and yet I'm grateful for my life for it has taught me to be appreciative of what I have, not focus on what I don't have. Even more, I'm grateful for not having worse challenges.

I'm also grateful to many experiences that I shared with you. Each and every one of them has many profound life lessons which carried me through those darkest days and shorten the length of those days. In each and every one of them bring me closer and closer to achieving my goals and dreams.

The purpose of the book is to show you how to survive and to put yourself out in the world by taking actions, so you can create a healthy, joyful, happiness, purposeful ... Life.

My childhood was hijacked. In my childhood, all I did was to survive. As I'm getting older, just surviving is not enough. I wanted to live the life of my dreams, purpose and desires.

The stories in this book are my true stories, but they are for the purpose of showing you examples to overcome challenges in using my strategies.

**Really, it's ALL about and for you. I want to share, show, and return to those like you.**

Life is very precious and fragile. Live it wisely. There is a price and limit to everything in life. Choose wisely what price to pay, make sacrifices and acceptant for your happiness, peace of mind, freedom, joy, health, wealth and everything else because it has the consequences, negative or positive, which you and those surrounding will have to face.

One of my goals is to get you to start awakening, stay alert, enjoying and living your dreams in the moment simply with what you have and wherever you are in life now; start recognizing and experiencing all that is possible; and start using all your gifts, all your abilities, and your secret happiness, peace of mind, freedom, joy, health and wealth to the maximum extent you're entitled to with no regret and without hurting/harming yourself and others along the way.

The lessons you soon will read have been shown to be scalable and applicable to just about anyone.

Still, will people apply these lessons? Will you?

I can neither predict nor control that. I'll send this letter to you with my prayer that in the process of weeding and applying, you will either find, regain, or strengthen your life, joy, happiness, peace of mind, health, freedom, compassion, prosperity, and purpose.

## Welcome!

## Chapter One

## Swimming Lessons From A Cow

Granted, to most people, standing in an open rice field while war planes are flying overhead would be considered a bad day. Sure, it's not like most people's typical bad days, but at that time in my life, it was typical enough that I knew what was happening and what I needed to do at a very young age.

We've all had bad days. You know the type. You wake up late, spill coffee on your favorite shirt, get stuck in traffic, or drop your iPhone and crack the screen. Naturally, I have those days, too. But when I do, I step back and realize that they are merely inconveniences—small, insignificant events that only have the power to wreck my day if I let them. In the grand scheme of the vast universe, they are just a grain of sand among the things that will shape our lives.

Everyone has had experiences that transform their lives—things that actually shape much more than how we view our day, but instead, provide us with a different perspective on life. My childhood in war-torn

Cambodia provided me with many such experiences, and although they weren't anything I'd actually wish for, I wouldn't trade any of them for a different life. The lessons I learned through those experiences have, in fact, led me to the life I live today—a big life full of gratitude, health, freedom, joy, happiness, peace of mind, and prosperity.

I think our perspective on life is modeled from our experiences. What may seem trivial and unimportant to some may seem monumental and catastrophic to others, depending on their previous experiences and life circumstances. A person who has had an easy life might be devastated when their bank account falls below six figures, while a person who has had hardships might feel grateful to simply be able to pay their bills. It's all about perspective, which comes from life lessons.

My first lesson actually came at a very young age. I was five years old and carrying out one of my tasks. In communist-controlled Cambodia, children were expected to do chores, not just at home, but for the government. One of my "jobs" was to bring the cows to their grassy feeding area.

Our home was in an area where there were days when the sky seemed to open up and dumped an ocean of water on the land, resulting in torrential downpours. Scientifically, it's called a monsoon. But from an observer's standpoint, it's basically a large outdoor swimming pool. There was standing water everywhere, stretching out to the horizon and everything you can see or touch was soaking wet. We've all seen puddles, but monsoons left puddles the size of Texas. There is no escaping them or going around them. One literally has to swim through them.

When the ground is covered with water and the earth is saturated to the hilt, grass cannot grow. So I had to cross the river of water to take the cow I was in charge of to grassy land on the higher ground. It wasn't an easy task for anyone, especially a five year old. Now, I could have gotten out of it by lying and saying I fed the cow, like when a child tells a little fib and says they brushed their teeth, but they didn't. But I knew better. I was responsible for the cow and feeding it was my job. The cow wasn't owned by my family or a neighbor. It was owned by the "Organization," or Angkar in Khmer. One might think that the Angkar wouldn't know or care whether the cow missed one feeding. Tell that to a five year old who likens their government to the mafia. When you mess with them, they will mess with you. I had that fear and wasn't about to test my luck. I was going to feed that cow, come hell or high water (pun intended). If I didn't, I feared they would "take care of" me or my family. That's a lot for a young girl to shoulder.

So I set off with my cow and started our trek across the river. I might have omitted one small detail—I didn't know how to swim. In fact, I was deathly afraid of the water. As I stood on the bank of the river, it was impossible not to notice the strong current as the swollen river rushed downstream. I looked across toward the grass and gauged my distance. Beyond frightened, I knew I was in deep trouble, but I also knew what I had to do. The cow wanted grass—I wanted to live. I very much wanted to quickly cross the river and be done with this job, but instead, I froze. Panicked, I couldn't bring myself to move. The cow, on the other hand, was a little smarter … and a lot braver than me.

The cow knew that it could swim. Unfortunately, the cow was the only one with that inside information. I had no clue that it could swim until it started swimming across the river. Left behind, I knew I had to act quickly! I couldn't lose the cow; it didn't belong to me—it belonged to the Angkar. Again, I didn't want to die. So I did the only thing I could do—I grabbed the cow by the tail and hung on for dear life. Yes, Heng hung on. There it is—I said it!

Have you ever held on to the tail end of the cow? Well, let me tell you, you can determine what it had for breakfast! Seriously, the smell is not very pleasant. But it was better than the alternative, which was dying. So while I was trying to feed the cow and care for it, it was reciprocating by inadvertently saving my life. I'm sure the scene would have been hilarious to onlookers. Sometimes, I imagine what it may have looked like from the sky—a helicopter flying overhead with its pilot doubled over in laughter as he watched a little five-year-old Cambodian girl floating down the river as she was hanging onto a swimming cow. At the time, though, there was nothing humorous about it. I was phobic about water and had no idea where the cow was going or where it would take me. Obviously, the cow did—and truthfully, even if it didn't, there was nothing I could do about it.

The cow obviously had its GPS on and found where it needed to go—it must be a natural instinct for animals to find food, even if they have to go over the river and through the woods. I don't think I was ever so relieved (again, pun intended) as I was when the cow stepped onto the bank. Solid land! I was ecstatic to be alive, and judging by the way the cow thrashed its tail back and forth, it was just as glad that I had let go.

I was safe, for the time being, but I was still scared. I was wet, cold, and my legs were weak. Sinking to the ground, I sat and watched the cow calmly and leisurely eat its lunch, as if nothing had happened. But I knew something significant and rich had happened, and my mind replayed the events one more time while I waited.

What really happened? Well, I did my job and saved myself from drowning and deep or even lethal punishment by the "Organization." But something even bigger than that happened. I was gifted a huge life lesson. However, it wasn't until I was older, in my teens, that I truly realized what that lesson was. It was one of those lessons that percolates until you're ready and then stays with you for life. Over time and many applications, I've come to call that lesson and model the S.B.C.I.A. It's an acronym for a five-step strategies for dealing with just about any challenge we are confronted with. It stands for: Stop, Breathe, Center, Inventory, and Action.

Let me explain. Whenever I'm confronted with a challenge, regardless how big or small it is, I tell myself to STOP! I stop everything and avoid any temptation to jump into fixing the situation. I remove myself from the scene and do nothing more than observe, just like an outsider would. STOP helps me to objectify because, as it's been said, "You can't read the label from inside the bottle." After I stop, then and only then, can I be present to the situation and effective.

The next step I take is to BREATHE. Naturally, this is important. We can't live without breathing, right? I'm pretty sure it would be hard to swim with a cow without taking a breath a time or two, as well. Breathing serves an important function here, which is to keep a person present in the moment. Think about it. You can't breathe in the past, and you certainly can't breathe in the future. You can only breathe in the present. When you do, it takes you out of the panic mode where you cannot think clearly, if at all, and keeps you in the present.

The C stands for CENTER. When you stop and breathe, you can calm down and become centered. It's an amazing feeling—when you're centered, you can actually feel yourself connected to the earth, your feet squarely on the ground. You lose that sense of spiraling out of control and the desire to scramble and run around in circles so you can focus on the matter at hand, which in this case was survival—for both me and the cow.

The fourth step is I, which stands for INVENTORY. Take an honest and objective inventory of the resources you have available to you at the moment. In my case, those resources were water, or more aptly stated, the momentum of the water. The next thing I had was fear. While some people may not consider fear to be a resource, but rather a detriment, fear has a purpose. Fear fuels energy. All I had to do was convert that energy into the fifth step: ACTION. Clearly, one major resource I had was a cow. I know I'm a minority with that one—not too many people have a cow as part of their inventoried arsenal in a time of crisis, but I did because it was a cow who had instincts of both need and desire. So therefore, this cow literally may have saved my life. And how did I make it back? Simple. With my newfound confidence in the cow and MYSELF, armed with the S.B.C.I.A. (which I didn't really know at a conscious level yet), I simply retraced my steps and returned from the job at hand as though I was victoriously returning from battle; the battle of my fears. Life changed for me that day, and I offer this lesson up to you to apply whenever and wherever it can upgrade your life, as well.

The next time you have a WTF (What The Freak) day, use S.B.C.I.A. and see how much difference it makes in your outcome. You have resources—thankfully, and they may even be better than a cow, a rushing river, and a panic attack. Face it. You have some amount of friends, books, information, technology, time, money, and experiences on your side. Take an inventory of what is available to you. When you do, what originally looks bleak and like a lost cause transforms itself into a workable situation. You can devise a plan to produce a different outcome than the one your imagination conjured, which is usually the worst-case scenario.

It's amazing how much difference it makes to stop, breathe, center, inventory, and take action when life throws you challenges. Suddenly, you see things from a different, far better, perspective, and your WTF transforms into OMG—Oh my God, look what I did! Look what I can do! I never thought I'd be capable of pulling a cow across a swollen, angry river; but then again, I never thought a cow would be capable of towing me across one, either.

Today, I can find humor in that situation, and I can literally laugh out loud as I recant the story. When I was five, I would have done anything, *anything,* not to have experienced such a harrowing incident. But today, knowing that I survived it and the lesson it taught me, I wouldn't trade the experience for anything. Because I swam with a cow, I have redefined the WTFs in my life. They are no longer shocking or scary. When I stop, breathe, center, and inventory, I can transform any WTF into "Wow, That's Fantastic!"

And I have a cow to thank for that.

Who do you have to thank for the transformational experiences in your life—those that mold you into a stronger, more grateful, and happier person? They're there … practice a little S.B.C.I.A. and you'll find them.

Chapter Two

## Fight, Flight, Or Chill

I have just a few memories of my father. It's been years since he's been gone, but the things I do remember about my dad and our time together will always be cemented in my memory bank. Rarely do I access them intentionally, though. They are usually spurred, quite unexpectedly, by circumstances beyond my control. Those that do come to me from time to time are profound and meaningful—they are the type of memories that dwell in my subconscious, seemingly forever, waiting for the opportunity to present themselves once again and recreate the impact they had the first time they were experienced. Today was no different.

Driving down California's freeway, I was making good time and enjoying the mild weather. With only a few scant clouds scattered across the sky, the sun was able to shine in its full glory, and I was enjoying my leisurely drive. I'd driven this stretch of road countless times and had timed my departure accordingly, knowing that traffic flowed rather smoothly in the early afternoon—between the busier lunch hour congestion and late afternoon swarm of commuters in a rush to get home after a long day at work. I was on my way to a business meeting I'd been looking forward to for some time. Using the time spent driving to mentally prep myself, I didn't even have the radio on. Instead, I had the window rolled down, enjoying the fresh air and the opportunity to think without interruptions. Today, it was important that I make a good impression, and I wanted to focus.

The car ahead of me tapped its brakes, once and then again. The third time, the brake lights stayed on as the car came to a slow, but steady, crawl, then stopped, taking its place at the rear of a long stretch of traffic—stopped traffic. Automatically, I glanced at the clock and mentally started gauging my time to determine if I was going to be late. Assured that I had a few minutes to spare, I sighed, realizing that there was absolutely nothing I could do … but wait.

A few minutes turned into a few more, and it became apparent that we weren't going anywhere soon. *It's a good thing I always choose to be early,* I thought, but the distant honking of horns told me that wasn't the case for everyone. *Everyone's in a hurry to get somewhere,* I observed, while my mind took a trip of its own.

*As a little girl, I was with my parents, back home in Cambodia. Khmer Rouge, the communist genocidal regime that had invaded and controlled our country for three years, eight months, and twenty days, had been ousted in 1979. We were liberated, they said. People were told they were free—free to travel, go home to their families, and visit their loved ones. It was exciting news, but most people, including my parents, were afraid to believe it. Was it true? What if it wasn't? Was it propaganda? Who, if anyone, could they trust? The uncertainty had gone on for days, before my parents finally decided to take a chance and we started walking toward my grandmother's village.*

*Dad had been very sick for some time, and my mom had been his caregiver and the sole supporter of our family. Being near our grandmother would give them the support and help they desperately needed. But we knew the trip wouldn't be easy, especially for my dad, who by this time, could only walk with extreme difficulty and the aid of a cane.*

*Ever so slowly, we set out across an open rice field. There wasn't a tree in sight—just acres and acres of rice fields. Some of the fields had been harvested, leaving behind the dark, bare earth, while acres of fields in various stages of gold fanned out in all directions, awaiting the laborers who would soon tend to their stalks. With rice fields as far as the eye could see, the walk promised to be long and trying.*

*Then, I heard the plane. Instinctively, I knew the sound—it was a war plane. Even though I was young, I knew what that meant—when a war plane flew over, bombs were certain to quickly follow. My mind and body automatically went into survival mode. I knew the drill.*

*Scared and frantic, I looked around for a place to hide, but there was nowhere to go. We were exposed and without shelter or cover. Panic kicked in, and I tried to make my dad move. "Dad, Hurry up! Faster! Faster!" I screamed, pushing him from behind to move forward. He didn't budge. Though I tried, I wasn't strong enough to help him along; it was like an ant trying to push an elephant. So I went around to the front and grabbed his hand, thinking that pulling him might be easier. Running from front to back, I pushed and pulled, yelling at him to hurry and walk faster, and I was angry at him for not being able to.*

*Then I heard the bombs explode. I'd known it was coming, and both the threat and fear of being hit had been very real. Thank goodness, though, it didn't hit close to us. We were spared, for if we had to run in order to save our lives, my dad wouldn't have been able to—he was far too sick and so very weak.*

The sound of a horn brought me back to the present. The traffic had just started to move again, and the impatient driver behind me tapped his horn to make me move. *Ironic,* I thought. *This time, I'm the one who is not moving and am making someone else uneasy.*

I pulled forward, matching the speed of the car ahead of me, but my mind hung back. The fear I had re-experienced had ebbed, but the image stayed clear—an image that replays in my mind from time to time, of the bombs falling and my dad standing there at the mercy of fate, not able to move at all when his life depended on it.

Life gives us many experiences, some of which invoke fear. My father was exposed to imminent danger, knowing he would not be able to save himself. Yet he showed no sign of fear. The only shelter he had was faith; it was invisible, but it was his only option. You see, Dad didn't discuss his faith too often with me. When he did it always revolved around his belief in a higher power, one which was boundless, all knowing, without limitation and with undying love, support, and protection for its believers. Therefore, he feared no man and no situation. Those were his beliefs, and they were based on his unwavering faith even under untenable circumstances.

Here in America, we enjoy relative freedom from fear of these sorts of challenges and atrocities as we go about our daily activities, but we are often exposed to difficult situations and circumstances that are beyond our total control. When that happens, the only thing we can really control is ourselves: our interpretations, emotions, and responses.

Sometimes there are situations that are not within our control. It might be as minor as a traffic jam or as devastating as an act of war. I learned at an early age that we can't always hide, from anyone or anything. There will be times when we are all in our own open field, completely exposed. We can push and pull with all of our might, but we know we are helpless and cannot escape the naked reality that we have nowhere to turn, but to that which we cannot see. It is then that we are forced to trust something bigger than ourselves and use that as our guide post.

It is our ego that believes that we are in total control of our lives and that we can hide behind our suits, our titles, makeup or money. Truth is, we are not in total control of anything, except our response to a person or situation. We cannot unjam traffic or hold our hands up and wish away a bomb. We cannot escape our past or our future. What will be, will be, whether we want it to be or not, and the true and certain path to pain is not accepting that.

The unexpected lurks around every corner, and we cannot do anything more than prepare for it, if possible. Sometimes, we have to trust that the outcome is not in our hands, but in a greater power—and it would be futile to try to change it. In those instances, just like my dad, I've learned to turn to faith, to a higher being. I've come to the realization that I cannot push people to do something or pull things along to make them happen according to my desires and wants. I simply do not have that strength, power, or ability. Whether I'm sitting in a traffic jam or totally exposed in a rice field during a time of war, I have to accept reality and know there is only so much I can do.

That's what my dad did. He didn't try to run or hide. He didn't throw himself to the ground or seek any protection from fate. He simply stood still and allowed what was going to happen to happen. Powerless to ward off or outrun an attack, he counted on something bigger than shelter for our survival. He turned to faith and did the only thing he could do, which in his case, was to accept life on its terms.

It wasn't really until many years later that I began to understand this lesson from my dad. And even today I find myself standing in the question of, "what can I change and what do I need to accept?" The greeting card, the serenity prayer addresses this age-old conundrum so it's not as though it's a "no brainer" issue. But the lesson to me has been to lean toward accepting what is, what realistically IS and letting go of my egoic propensity to control.

## Chapter Three

### Stormy, Stormy Night

The roaring and swift stream of water that I navigated with the help of that cow I mentioned earlier was the result of the monsoon season. During this time of the year, it would feel like the bottom fell out of the sky and literally dumped an ocean of water on top of the land. As one would expect, such torrential downpours were accompanied by the violent sounds of a dark and angry sky. The roar of thunder and cracks of lightning frequently broke through the sound of the pounding rain and the force of the wind.

When I was about five years old during that bloody Khmer Rouge Regime, my mom and dad had to go to a meeting after a long day at work. My father had retired from his job by the time the Regime took charge and was quite ill; he was mobile and functional, but ill, nonetheless. Still, he was required by the Regime to attend regular meetings which were held far away from our home. During those meeting times, I would stay behind at home … and alone because kids were not allowed to attend any of the meetings. I recall one particular night vividly—monsoon season had just begun and heavy rains fell from the dark skies while the wind howled around our house. Being so young, I naturally was frightened, and every sound, from the rain pounding on the roof to the wind roaring against the outside walls, increased my certainty that the house was going to collapse.

I should mention that I was afraid of the dark. In fact, along with the fear of swimming, or rather the fear of drowning, it was one of my deepest phobias. Afraid might not be the right word—I was actually petrified. It was pitch dark outside and inside, blacker than black, and I couldn't see my hand in front of my face, although that was partly because I was afraid to open my eyes. Every time the thunder roared, it shook the entire house. Knowing that there would be lightning to follow, I would squeeze my eyes shut in fear. Like a little rat, I tried to hide from Mother Nature's vengeance, but there was nowhere to go. I could not escape the storm, my fears, or the demons that, in my imagination, were certain to come and get me.

Folks used to say that there was a bird that made a weird sound like an owl, although it wasn't a Hoot! Hoot! noise. This sound was very, very scary and eerie. Legend had it that these birds made those sounds only in the darkness of night, when they could arrive undetected and wreak havoc and destruction. It was believed that these birds were sent by the devil for one reason—to take people's lives. If the sound of the bird was heard, it meant that somebody was going to die. Now, the story of that evil bird haunted me, even before that night and the storm it brought. But add the fear of hearing that bird to the abject terror a five-year-old suffers while being left alone during a dark and horrific storm, and you can imagine my state of mind. I was frozen in fear, afraid to move and afraid to open my eyes because I didn't want to see—I didn't want to see what was going to get me, what was going to happen to me. I didn't want to see a bird, the house falling in from all sides, or the ghosts that lurked in the dark and evil shadows.

I tried to hide under the bed, but there wasn't room. There were no corners or spots I could tuck myself into that would provide any semblance of cover, protection, or comfort. It was a long night—one I spent curled into a ball, afraid to move a muscle for fear that the ghosts, birds, and death would find me. Afraid to open my eyes, I was also frightened of what I couldn't see, so I was torn between tightly squeezing my eyes shut and ever so slightly opening just one to make sure the demons had not found me.

My salvation was my will to live, as well as my relatively newfound resources of the S.B.C.I.A. strategy.

After that scary ordeal, I did survive and live to share this with you. The ghosts and demons kept their distance until my parents returned and brought back with them my safety and security. I had survived! Even though I was sure death was calling my name, I never actually heard it. Maybe the wind and rain overpowered it, but I didn't care, as long as I had survived.

I'm not alone. I know that many young children have similar fears—they're afraid of the dark, scared of monsters under the bed, and frightened of storms. It's a natural response to the unknown. Both children and adults don't like dark moments, when they're afraid of what could happen, even though it may never well come to be. And when we are faced with fears, we don't like to be alone. We long for the comfort and assurance that everything is going to be all right and someone is by our side.

There are times in everyone's life when there will be darkness and things look bleak and beyond despair. These are the storms of our lives—whether we consider them to be monsoons, tornadoes, or hurricanes. Many are real. They could be the loss of a relationship or a job. For some, it could be health issues, not knowing where their next meal is going to come from, perhaps financial or even legal problems. And while many are real, there are many others that are simply not real. They are conjured in our minds but seem as real as gravity. While they are happening, they make us want to hide and search for shelter from the storm. These instances aren't reserved for children; adults, too, have very real fears and challenges. The storms we face can be very dark and frightening.

In the challenges and mess during the storms in our lives, we cannot always control what will happen. The one thing we can control is how we handle the situation in the moment. I've learned that we cannot always run and hide—there isn't always a quick fix or way out. Sometimes, we have to weather the storm, holding onto faith and the hope that we'll still be standing when it's over.

Have you ever had your electricity go out? The house suddenly goes still and quiet and very, very dark. It's at that moment that you appreciate light and power—the very things that you probably take for granted each and every day of your life. Only when it's gone and you have no guarantee if and when it will come back do you begin to appreciate it.

What other things do you take for granted? How about a relationship? You think it will always be there, until one day you hit a bump and it becomes rocky. Maybe you take a job for granted or the meal on your table. Regardless, I've learned when it's gone or threatened in any way, that's when we appreciate it the most.

Don't wait until the things that mean the most to you are gone before you begin to appreciate them in your life. Because of the storms I've endured and the fears that came with them, I've learned to be grateful for what I do have at any given point in my life. Even if I was hungry and my only meals consisted of a small bowl of porridge twice a day, I actually began to appreciate that mush.

Whenever storms challenge you, your livelihood, relationships, finances, or health, remember that you still have something to be grateful for. Everyone does. Here's an exercise that has helped me and others. Try it on. Starting today, make a list of seven things that you're grateful for and to a certain extent might be taking for granted. Create this gratitude list every day for seven days. You'll begin to have a different outlook on challenging situations. Instead of seeing the glass as half empty, you'll see that it is half full. That's because gratitude not only gives us more of the things we are grateful for, but it also reinforces our faith—the faith that things won't always be this dark and bleak, we won't always be alone, and this storm, too, shall pass.

The only thing we can control is how we respond when storms erupt. Being grateful keeps the demons, especially those that are imagined, at bay so we can see things clearly, without fearing what might, but probably won't, happen. Then we'll be able to open our eyes so we can see the light at the end of the tunnel when it shines … and it will.

Sometimes, our greatest fears are in times of darkness. By the light of day, we can look back and see that they weren't so scary, after all. And maybe, just maybe, we'll actually be grateful for the storms in our lives for making us stronger and teaching us vital lessons that will help prepare us to handle the next storm with grace, faith, and courage. And remember, do that gratitude list every day for the next seven days. It's a game changer!

## Chapter Four

**Dad And Princess**

I may have painted a negative picture of my early years, and by now, you probably have a rather bleak picture of my childhood, but I do have a few memories filled with content and happy moments. As a young child, I wasn't much different than most kids. Sure, I had to work for the "Organization," but it was the only life I really knew. It's true that you don't really miss what you never had.

At one point in our lives, my parents had a very nice home and they were considered wealthy by some because my father previously worked for the government in the role of authorizing people to enter Cambodia. He had power and authority. He earned good money and provided well for his family, but that family wasn't actually mine.

It's important that you understand that the nice house I refer to wasn't one I grew up in. You see, my mom's parents were farmers and they had eight children of their own. When my mother was just eight years old, her father passed away, leaving her mom as the sole support for all of the children. At the time, my mom was staying with her aunt and helping her. When her father died, she never went back home. Her aunt had a friend who then took my mom in at the young age of eight and paid her to help around their house. In essence, she was an eight-year-old servant. The money she made was sent back to her mother to help support her siblings. While it may sound rather cold and cruel to allow an eight year old to be a servant, the woman was very good and kind to my mom. In fact, she treated my mother as if she were her own daughter. Over time, they forged a close bond and relationship.

Then, things began to change. You see, my dad was married to that woman. As my mom grew into her mid-teens, he, too, became fond of my mom, but in a different way. My mom realized that my father was starting to like her, and it left her feeling more than a little unsettled. For one thing, he was married, and to a woman who was dear to my mom. He was also quite a bit older than my mother. He was an adult with a wife and kids of his own, and by most accounts, my mom was also a kid. As a result of this, to put it bluntly, my mom began to hate him. She simply wanted no part of his interest.

My dad was persistent and not one to give up easily. He began leaving my mom secret notes, money, and gifts. My mom's loyalties, however, resided with his wife. Plus, she was very disgusted by this older, married man's disrespectful advancements. After all, she knew that if she wasn't a poor servant to be exploited, he'd never make advances in that manner. Because of that, she did what she felt was the only proper and appropriate thing to do—she gathered all of the money, notes, and gifts he'd given her and presented it all to his wife, thus exposing his advances to my mom. As one can imagine, it didn't end well. Situations such as these may be where the phrase "never underestimate the anger of a woman scorned" originated. The fact that she was angry wasn't lost on anyone, especially after the woman grabbed a gun and started shooting at her husband for betraying her.

But still, this woman stayed married to my father, and my mom continued working for them. This went on for a few years, before my mom finally decided that she simply couldn't continue to live there under those circumstances. She moved out, but she didn't go back home to her family. She still needed to work and earn money to help her mom. By this time, she was an experienced servant and had no difficulty finding another employer to take her in. It was while my mom was living with this family that her former employer, my father's wife, passed away.

Once his wife was gone, my father was even more persistent in his efforts to court my mom. He used every opportunity he had to attempt to see her. Ironically, it wasn't his charm or persistence that won her over. It was her sense of loyalty and duty. My mom finally agreed to pay him a visit, six years later —not because she liked him or was warming to him at all, but because an elderly lady who knew them begged my mom to visit him, saying he was so sick that he might not make it. To put it bluntly, she felt sorry for him. It was pity, loyalty and duty, not love, that actually wore my mom down.

Of course, their relationship didn't even remotely resemble 'love at first sight.' On the contrary, it took several more years before my mom warmed up to him, felt a connection in her heart, and finally agreed to marry my father. Out of obligation to his former wife and a lot of pity, my mom began taking care of my father, whose health was very much on the decline. Over time, she warmed to him, although she certainly made him work for her affections. Mom told me that my father joked about it from time to time, taking pride in his persistence and the fact that my mom wasn't an easy catch. They were total opposites. She was quite young, and my father, well, he was quite a bit older. My mom had never received a formal education of any kind, but she was rather street smart. My dad, on the other hand, was rich and educated. While my father hadn't exactly robbed the cradle, today, the relationship between an older government official and a young, uneducated servant would spark some scrutiny, as well as a tabloid headline or two.

My mother knew that my father had once been a wealthy man. She was also aware that he was pretty much broke before she married him. However, it wasn't until after they were married that she learned just how much debt he actually had. Creditors were coming to the house on a daily basis demanding payment. In order to pay off the debt, my mom had to sell many of his first wife's belongings, which, given her admiration and close relationship with her, wasn't an easy task. She shared with me that it was quite emotional and painful. Again, my mom did what she had to do for the benefit of her family—a trait that she has exhibited during her entire life.

My mom and dad lived together in the same house where my mother was once a servant. Like I said, it was a very nice home, and my parents rather took pride in it. Then the Khmer Rouge Regime took control. With control of the government, they also took control of people's lives and homes. They told people where they would live, work, and what they would eat. The food that we grew or bought was replaced by rations from the "Organization," which consisted mostly of porridge.

Because of my father's old age and the fact that he was sick even before he married my mother, the memories I have of him are few. During the Khmer Rouge Regime, when I was about five years old, my father and I were alone one evening. I was like most little girls—I had an imagination and loved to play and pretend. One of my favorite pastimes was pretending to be a beautiful princess—doesn't every girl want to be a princess? We all had our own fairy tales, and it was no secret that that one was mine. One particular night, I was eating my supper, and I can remember my dad saying, "Daughter, every princess, every pretty princess eats all her rice on the plate." At that moment, there were a few pieces of rice on my plate. As soon as those words came out of his mouth, I picked up every piece of rice on my plate and ate them all, leaving my plate spotless. From that moment until today, every single time I eat a meal, I hear his voice as a reminder to eat all of the food on my plate, if at all possible. Not just because my dad tricked me into it, but because I knew that it was one of his ways of loving me, supporting that part of me that would become very important in my survival through very difficult times under the dictatorship of Cambodia … my imagination!

I'm so grateful for this memory of my dad and the fact that his words had a major impact on my life. But there is another reason why it has left such a lasting and profound imprint. As I was talking to my mother and reminiscing about that day, my mom mentioned that so many of my countrymen were starving during the Regime. Food was not to be taken lightly, and anything one could get was worthy of appreciation. Only once per month were we served rice as you and I know it to be—regular rice which has substance that you can chew. The standard, daily rice meal we were served was the porridge, that soft and mushy kind. As I think about it, my father wasn't eating alongside me, because he had given me his portion. While he was sick and hungry, still he sacrificed even the small portion he had for the sake of his daughter, his Princess. For this he asked for nothing, only that I didn't waste any of it. With this, he imbued a very important lesson to me; give with an open heart and where sharing is its own reward. And while I certainly was grateful for my father's sacrifice, I took away the lesson of appreciation; the attitude of gratitude. Clearly he was a loving and generous man who unquestionably acted altruistically with his family and others, and I may have taken that for granted, thinking that that's what all fathers did. My appreciation then for Dad was nothing compared to my appreciation of him now.

It is a lesson I will carry with me for the rest of my life. I equate it to being present and appreciating everything I have in life, taking nothing for granted. Even if your only meal is a spoonful of plain rice, it should be appreciated as much as filet mignon. It's about appreciating what you already have, rather than feeling empty or longing for what you don't have or what is missing in your life.

It's an attitude of gratitude, one that can truly be understood at its deepest level by those who have the very least. Instead of being upset that you don't have the job of your dreams, be thankful for the job you do have and take action on getting that dream job of yours. It's about appreciating what life has to offer now, in the present moment, and not letting yourself be discouraged when it's offering less than expected. When that appreciation is exercised and fully implemented in our lives, it serves as a reminder of the blessings we do have, no matter how big or small.

I know that there is no such thing as "too little" and will always be grateful for the things life has given me, from a few grains of rice to a father's inspirational words to his dreamy-eyed daughter. At the time, they might not have seemed like very much, but now I know just how meaningful they both were. I am eternally grateful for these lessons and what they taught me. Mostly, though, I am grateful for the man who sacrificed for his princess in order to teach important lessons to me.

## Chapter Five

**A Meal To Remember**

I remembered my father's words as he encouraged me, his princess, to finish all of the food on my plate. But I don't actually remember the food or how it tasted or smelled. During the entire Regime, which lasted three years, eight months, and twenty days, there was only one meal I vividly really remember eating.

We were at the central location—the place everyone walked to for their daily meal allotments, knowing that there was no other way to get food. That food wasn't free—we had to work for it. If one didn't work, one didn't get to eat. Not only would the person goes hungry, but failing to work would also result in punishment. If you didn't contribute in any way, you were not only replaceable, but also disposable. Not doing what was expected made you a burden on the "Organization." To them, removing the burden was not a loss. With that mindset, the people who tested their limits and refused to do as told were very few and far between.

The entire village would gather for their lunch and dinner. There were three groups, and each had a designated area—the men, women, and children were always separated during meals. I took my place in line. The food, again, was rice soup, or what we referred to as porridge. It didn't have much flavor or nutrition, for that matter. I remember looking at this meal, seeing a watered down version of what could have been soup, but fell short. The rice was so scarce I could barely see it, and the only vegetable swimming in the tasteless broth was watercress. On the bright side, there was one piece of fish about the size of the fingernail on my pinkie floating on the top of liquid that was an unappetizing purple-brown color that defies description.

This was the meal that I worked to be privileged to receive. It wasn't the meal given to those who were being punished—this was our only source of nutrition and sustenance. I'd go to work in the morning and do my "chores," like feeding cows, and I'd be able to eat. If I didn't work, I didn't eat. After each meal, I had to go to work again to earn the next one.

Because I was hungry, I ate all of it, even though it didn't look or taste very good. After I ate, I remember still being hungry. We all were. My mom has told me that there were times my father was so hungry that he needed to get creative. He would take the basket that was used daily to get his ration of rice, leave it in the sun to dry out, and then shake it to expose any grains of rice that got stuck in the woven palm leaf basket. Being so hungry after having such a minimal amount of food, this was his way of making the most out of his situation and he ate every single grain available. The man was so hungry and underfed. It saddens me to think back on this. However, the lesson is one that will stay with me forever; waste not, want not. Appreciate everything. Be grateful.

Of course, I didn't know it at the time, but we experienced what would be referred to as clinical starvation—not simply hunger. This was a real gnawing hunger that never was satisfied. I saw my father waste away and become a shell of his former self as a result of starvation, and I know it also had an effect on my physical growth. Because I grew up in such a harsh time and in conditions where everyone was subjected to extreme poverty, my growth was actually stunted due to lack of nutrition during the formative years of my life.

The scarcity I experienced in my childhood has developed and reinforced my attitude of gratitude. Because I know the alternative, good health is a priority in my life. I always try to eat well and exercise. The foods I choose have nutritional value; they aren't empty calories, for I learned long ago how important the right foods are to my physical and emotional wellbeing. Of course, today I have many more options than watered-down porridge, but I let myself recall that one meal from time to time, because I want to be thankful for the food I do have, even if it might not be what I prefer at that moment.

I also apply this lesson to other things in my life. If I have a quarter, I'm grateful for it, even if, deep down, I wish it was a dollar. And I spend it wisely, choosing not to squander it on something that has no value or substance. Growing up hungry and sometimes literally starving taught me many lessons, one of which is the difference between good habits and bad habits. You see, bad habits have no positive value whatsoever because they actually stunt a person's mental, emotional, or physical growth. Good habits, however, support our growth and nurture our mind, body, and soul. They feed us with the proper physical, mental and emotional nutrition to live a productive, positive life and can literally facilitate our transformation from internment to fulfillment.

I must admit that sometimes it saddens me to see people waste food in restaurants. More than once, I found myself in judgment about that—feeling like food was being taken for granted, I wanted to go over and remind people how fortunate we are to have such abundance, while there are people today who go to bed hungry in so many nations, including our own. I never followed through and stood on a soapbox … till now that is, with sincere hopes that people will read my story about our starvation and the heroic sacrifices that my dad made for me to have enough food at the expense of his own hunger and health.

I hope people will be more appreciative and respectful of the food before them, make smart choices of food, in terms of nutritional value and not just taste, and perhaps share food with others less fortunate. Okay, off my soapbox for now.

## Chapter Six

**Choosing Paths**

It was a typical warm afternoon. I was about six years old and was on my way to the work for my evening meal. I was by myself because my parents were still at work, but I knew the way well, having taken that same path many times before. That path went through the heavy and green rice fields and was raised above water. I knew it well because it was the only route back and forth from our house to our next meal.

As I embarked across the path, I saw a dog lying across it up ahead. The first thing I noticed was that this dog had a stump where its tail had once been. Now, it was common belief among our people that dogs without tails were crazy. Call it what you will, a suspicion, wives' tale, or myth … but in my six-year-old mind, I had no reason to question it. It was a "truth."

In reality, though, it wasn't the fact that the dog had no tail that caused it to be labeled "crazy." The truth is, cutting off a dog's tail was supposedly a cure when the dog exhibited signs of being unstable or vicious. So, the fact of the matter is that the dog had behavioral problems which then led to its tail being chopped off.

At the time, I didn't know all of that—I just knew that a tailless dog was one to stay far away from. But I had to eat … and there wasn't an alternate route for me to take. The path was my one and only option. So I kept walking, very, very slowly in an effort not to disturb the dog. As I came closer, I moved to the very edge of the path—the dog's body covered all but a very slim portion on the side of the path, and it showed no signs of moving. It didn't make a sound as I approached. It didn't bark or show any signs of friendliness or defensiveness.

Able to get a better look at the dog, I noticed that it had an infection on its rear end. Now I was dealing with a crazy dog that had no tail and an infection. So many thoughts and fears were whirring through my mind that my heartbeat felt like it would burst through my chest. But I remained as quiet as I possibly could, taking each step ever so slowly and gingerly. I kept my eyes straight ahead, taking great care to avoid looking into the dog's eyes, avoiding both eye and physical contact with the animal.

I made it past the dog and somehow managed to avoid even brushing up against it. Just when I thought I'd escaped any danger, the dog leaped up from behind me high enough to get a solid bite of my right ear. Immediately blood started gushing out onto my shoulder. Saying I was scared to death was an understatement; I was petrified, alone, and had no idea how bad my injury was. On top of that, I was in pain. It hurt to get bitten by a dog, and scary as heck when bitten by one that was downright crazy.

When my parents found out, they tended to my wound, but food wasn't the only thing that was scarce during the Regime—we also didn't have access to any medicine or antibiotics. My parents had to resort to home remedies, and in this case, the remedy they used was just as painful, if not more so, than the actual injury. Tips of sweet potato leaves were ground up with tobacco to form a salve that they applied to my earlobe. It felt like acid had been poured on my flesh.

The wound by itself wasn't serious. In time, it healed without inflicting any serious or permanent disfigurement or infection. However, it was the internal feelings and fears that lingered and left a lasting imprint in my mind. I was scared, and my father was livid, not with the dog, but with the dog's owner. I was the apple of his eye, and he was angry with the dog's owner for not controlling or containing the animal and allowing it to attack his little girl. But because the owner was a leader of the Regime, there was absolutely nothing he could say or do about it. Can you imagine my dad's frustration?

To this very day, I have a phobia about dogs and will avoid getting close to one at any cost. I don't care how friendly I'm told it is. It might be the best behaved dog in the universe, and I won't trust it or go anywhere near it. The wound has healed, but the fear has never subsided. Significant emotional events leave lasting impressions, especially painful ones.

It's hard to overcome fears when something bad happens in our lives. Traumatic experiences scar us internally, not externally. Sometimes, it is difficult, maybe impossible, to overcome the damage that is caused. For example, if someone is in an abusive relationship, they might leave, but come back again … and again and again. Finally, they give up, declaring their abuser as the winner. In other words, they stop trying to get away and accept that there is nothing they can do about it. If there is one thing I learned from being bitten by a crazy dog, it's that I don't have to be bit again. I don't have to put myself in a position where I'm subject to pain or fear. At the first sign of either, I prefer to walk away because I know the closer I allow myself to get, the more likely it is that I'll be in danger.

Maya Angelou once said, "People will forget what you said, people will forget what you did, but people will never forget how you made them feel." That is so true. When people make you feel good, you want to be closer to them. On the other hand, when people make you feel uneasy, scared, or inferior, you don't forget it. It's not a good feeling. But in this case there is a remedy—there is another path. As a six-year-old child, I couldn't avoid that dog. Today there are some situations that I find myself in that I simply cannot avoid, but as long as I'm consciously awake, aware and able, I will always avoid situations, relationships, and people that are negative or potentially dangerous. I avoid them at all costs and, when confronted by them, I simply walk away. I don't need to get bit by too many wild dogs to learn that one.

I use my discernment to see the truth, then I decide to walk away or confront the situation outweigh your battle. Is it worth fighting for?

So let me ask you, how many times have you awakened to the realization that a relationship, friendship, or even a job was just not serving your higher purpose? Consider this; you will continue to attract these situations until you wake up the scent of those crazy dogs and take an alternate path. When you do, you save yourself a lot of drama and trauma, not to mention potentially a bloody ear, and the medical bills that go along with it!

Chapter Seven

## The Khmer Rouge Regime

In everything, there is both good and bad. Cambodia is no different. The country I remember was beautiful, with its landscape marked by lush rice fields that resembled a quilt of greens. The people were industrious hard workers; among them were many farmers, as well as those who were educated, like my father, and had held jobs in business or as teachers or government officials. Then, the Khmer Rouge Regime invaded our country 1975 and punished those who were educated. Cambodians lost their jobs and their homes—they worked for the "Angkar" or "The Organization," one that ruled with oppression. Everyone, even children, had a job, even though it wasn't a job they were trained to do. After the takeover, communal farming became Cambodians source of survival.

Survival was the ultimate goal. I recall my mom telling me a few years after we arrived in the U.S.A. that the "Organization," through a ruse, told the people that they had to leave their homes for just three nights. They were assured that they would be allowed to return to their homes in a very short time, therefore, it wasn't necessary for them to take any of their belongings. When the capital city, Phnom Penh, was emptied, the Regime took over the houses, as well as the personal belongings and assets within them. It referred to itself as the "Angkar" or "The Organization." Everything belonged to Angkar. Our form of currency was also abolished, making any money Cambodians did have worthless. I can recall seeing paper money lying on the road and blowing in the wind. Not a soul scampered to pick it up because it had no value at all.

Gone were their homes, money, private property, jobs, and livelihoods. Farmers were the only exception—they were still allowed to farm; however, their land was taken over by the "Organization." Not only were they allowed to farm, but they were forced to do so, as were many former professionals and business people and children. Any faith they had was internal—religion was also abolished, and people understood that there would be dire consequences if they worshipped openly.

Those who refused to comply with the restrictions and demands of the "Organization" were tortured, imprisoned, or executed.

On April 17th, 1975 the day we were forced to evacuate from Phnom Penh —a very bad day—there was a big stream of people walking in one direction, guided by Pol Pot's soldiers, the communist Khmer Rouge. A man was walking—which would be okay if he had been walking with his bicycle in the right direction. But he wasn't. He caught the attention and sparked the anger of one of the bosses, who told him that he walking the wrong way. The man just kept walking, which spurred a tragedy that to this day is still beyond my comprehension.

When I told my mom my recollections a few years ago, she was shocked that I remembered it. She said the man had a purpose and needed to get home, one that any person with a soul would understand.

Despite the unstableness of our country and the poverty that befell its citizens, it had been a good morning for that man. He had a wonderful family, a wife and two sons who were nine years apart in age. The older son was around 14 years old. Like most children, he had to go to school. The younger boy, a beautiful five-year-old child, had a sore throat that day and was feeling a bit under the weather.

Their meager breakfast didn't curtail their love for each other and the joy the family found in spending time together. On this particular morning, they'd reminisced about their grandmother who had always tried to tell them stories, but due to her stuttering, they never came out quite right. Laughing and smiling through their meal, they honored their grandmother before heading out of the house to begin their day's work. On this day, the young boy stayed behind as a precaution to make sure he wasn't coming down with strep throat.

The father walked to work—the same as he'd done every day. Then, he was approached by another man who said he needed to speak with him. "What is it?" he asked. "Is everything all right with your family? The man replied, "My family is fine, but as I walked past your house, I heard crying. I assume it was your young boy and that he might be afraid or hurt."

Memories of their morning sprang into the man's mind. He thanked the man for letting him know and told him that his son had a sore throat, but their laughing that morning probably made it feel worse. "He probably laughed so hard he made himself sick," he joked. "I'll go check on him."

That's what he was doing. He turned around and headed in the opposite direction to tend to his son, a small smile on his face while he envisioned holding and comforting his son—and turning his tears back into laughter. He didn't get very far at all before someone yelled, "Where are you going?"

"I ..."

That was the only word that came out of his mouth. The only word. He was stopped dead in his tracks by a single bullet to the head. He wasn't given a chance to provide an explanation. He wasn't offered an opportunity to apologize or given a reprieve or a lesser punishment. His only crime was being a loving and devoted parent, and for that … for tending to the wellbeing of his little boy … he paid the ultimate price. He lost his life in one of the most barbaric and senseless killings I've had the heartache to witness.

Life is fragile. In the hands of monsters, young people with guns, power, and an absence of values, you never know what will happen. But I can tell you that you don't forget it when it does. Believe me, the sound of bullets and the terror and shock of watching a good, vibrant, and *innocent* man take his last breath does not go away. It haunts you. It traumatizes you. And it frightens you into submission, even if you're only five years old.

That was a tough day for everyone, especially for a five year old like me who had never seen anyone getting their eye blown out before. All it takes is one such incident to keep the masses in line and under control. That'll give you an idea of the flavor of the country at that time. Unfortunately, it was not the only incident of its kind that I witnessed.

How does an "Organization" entity create such oppression? It's actually not difficult to understand. First, you use force; in the case of the Khmer Rouge Regime, that meant creating civil war among the people. Then, you abolish their form of currency, rendering them impoverished and dependent on the "Organization" for survival. Any attempt to voice disapproval or dissent of the "Organization" or its policies resulted in death.

The one thing that the "Organization" feared the most was education and educated people. They preferred to rule over the illiterate, reasoning that they would not have the intelligence or ability to figure out what was going on. The Khmer Rouge wanted people to be ignorant of what was taking place. They forced people to be submissive and made accept their ideology without question.

But Cambodia had educated people—people who didn't trust the "Organization." They learned quickly that revealing any sign of intelligence put them in grave danger.

Afraid of being persecuted, Cambodians hid their education backgrounds. Business people were moved to the outskirts of the villages and became farmers. They spoke only the native tongue, Khmer, knowing that anyone who had an accent or spoke a foreign language would be labeled an intellectual. Even something as simple as wearing eyeglasses or having light skin could be detrimental to one's safety and well-being.

In essence, Cambodia, which was once a thriving country, was returned to the Stone Ages. The people were silenced, and their homes and families were ripped apart. Everyone, regardless of class, was thrown into dire poverty. The educated were tortured, imprisoned, and executed. Women and children were not spared among the dead. Individuals and whole families died from execution, starvation, disease, and overwork. There were as many as 1.5 to 2 million Cambodians who lost their lives during the Regime. The exact number of people who died during the Khmer Rouge reign of terror was not known due to the lack of records before Pol Pot took over the country. Sadly, there were many who died without graves; some graves may never be discovered because trees were planted on top of them as part of their cover up.

While I was just a child, the torture, poverty, and fear were evident, even at my young age and naiveté. My parents could not hide these things from me—I, like all children, was taught to understand that I was expected to obey the "Organization" and carry out my duties. In order to survive, I had to understand that the consequences for refusing were very serious and very real.

At the age of five, I worked full time. There was no school. Everyone had to work; there were absolutely no exceptions. Even those who were very ill, like my father, were expected to labor for the "Organization." Along with feeding and caring for the cows, I also had to carry heavy waterlogged rice seedlings. I delivered them to the women, whose job was then to plant them. We didn't dally, but instead did as we were told, without argument.

We were staying at my grandmother's house, where she used to live in the village. Because of our family history, we were treated very badly. Everyone knew my father was an educated man, and so was my older stepbrother. We all paid the price for their education.

We didn't live like an educated or well-to-do family. In fact, we were as poor as everyone else. The entire nation lived without electricity and amenities, without exception. We all feared the "Organization." We never talked at night, because the Angkar would spy on people in an attempt to overhear any tidbit of information that could pose a threat to them. If one talked about the "Organization," they would be punished or killed. They also attempted to listen and learn if anyone indicated any signs of being educated.

Even our clothing was controlled. Everyone had to wear black clothing from head to toe—wearing black indicated that we accepted the "Organization's" policies and would be subservient to them. Even the shoes were black, which were made from car tires. Dying our clothes and making our shoes were also some of my jobs. Well, the shoe job lasted as long there were enough tires for us to create them! The shoes were for Angkar. The rest of the people, including me, were barefoot. I also had other jobs, including chopping trees, which were then to be used as fertilizer for the rice fields. In the summer when harvesting was done, I would have to pick up cow pies, which I would then pound into small pieces for use as fertilizer. Clearly, work was diverse, depending upon the season and what the Angkar needed. We never knew. We just did what we were told. Any job we had to do, whether difficult, smelly, filthy or whatever, we did it. No matter what, I was going to get myself from internment to fulfillment, cow pies or not!

The jobs were so very diverse. In addition to planting and harvesting rice, watermelon, and cucumbers, I also had to hunt rabbits. I was the last one in the group to reach the rabbits because I was the smallest and couldn't run as quickly as everyone else. Our hunt became part of our communal meal. When I say communal meal, I mean just that. We were not permitted to prepare and eat meals in our hut. If you do so, you could end up getting you cooked. They were not kidding around.

While I worked, I grew to enjoy the beautiful nature in our country. At times, there was a quiet and peaceful feeling that contradicted the torture and killing that was commonplace. The water was crystal clear, and I could see frogs, fish swimming, and crabs and snails crawling at the bottom. I remember vividly birds creating their nests. These are the good memories that I still hold to this day.

I'm often astounded at how vivid some of my recollections are, given my young age at the time. There was no schooling. I didn't play—I didn't even have toys. The truth is, I was a rather quiet child who preferred to watch the other children, rather than join them. Maybe it was because I was so small, and maybe it was fear that held me back and kept me afraid from doing anything I wasn't told to do. I didn't want to push my luck or test the seriousness of the threats that surrounded us daily.

My childhood was certainly not a privileged or carefree one. Unlike so many children, I learned the true value of living at a very young age. People often ask me what tool or mechanism I used to 'get by' during these times, and very often I find myself answering with the F word … FAITH; oh, and the H word ... Hope. Both were big parts of my survival.

Acceptance was my strategy. It was an inner attitude of compliance and knowing that outwardly questioning authority would have very grave repercussions. I learned to focus inward on what I was doing, but not the fact that I had to do it. Inwardly, I kept the end goal in mind, which was doing each job right and getting it done.

Survival is a mindset, whether you're a small child growing up in a communist-ruled country or you're suffering through other serious personal or professional issues. I was powerless to change our circumstances. The worst thing I could have done was to outwardly question or defy authority. If I had, I would have subjected myself and possibly my entire family to torture or death.

There was but one way to stay alive—by being strong enough to accept our fate for as long as necessary. I wore the armor of faith, with the confidence that it would protect me. I clung to the inner faith that I would survive, and that this, too, shall eventually pass—that was my salvation. I liken this mindset to the Serenity Prayer, which describes principles that have guided so many people in their darkest times:

God grant me the serenity to accept the things I cannot change;

courage to change the things I can;

and wisdom to know the difference.

We might not have been able to worship or practice our religion openly, but there is no denying that those who survived the Khmer Rouge Regime had one very strong force on their side—their faith.

As I think back, I can trace my values of hope, faith, service to others, courage, resilience and others to these early childhood experiences.

What are your highest values and where in your life did you learn them. I have hope and faith in you that you will make a list of your highest values and keep that list close to you; in your wallet, posted on your mirror and be able to recite them from memory. For, as it's been said, "when the values are clear, the decisions are easy". This is another example of how I've applied the S.B.C.I A. strategy because after you do your S.B. and C. (stop, breathe and center) then you will want to I. (inventory) your values each and every time before you begin to A (act). Yet, in order to easily access your values during the I. stage, it's important that you have them memorized for quick and easy access. It seems that the most successful people and companies that I see are values based, live and conduct business base activities with their values in mind. In fact, a long-term study was referenced by Dr. Ken Blanchard, noted co-author of *The One Minute Manager and Raving Fans*, which revealed businesses with values clearly written in their mission statements were extremely more profitable than those who didn't.

You, too, will enjoy the peace, prosperity, and freedom from fear when you hold these values in the front of your mind and lead your life in harmony and integrity with them. Liberation through values-based living. Yes!

## Chapter Eight

## Death Hits Home

One thing I learned at a young age was that death is not a particular moment or event. It's a process in most cases. In reality, my father had been dying for years before he actually passed away. While his health was continually declining, he suffered the loss of his son.

My father had two sons and a daughter from his first marriage. My youngest half-brother, of whom I have very little memory, had been sent far away from home to work. He became very ill with malaria and eventually had to be admitted to a makeshift hospital. It wasn't really a hospital—there were no doctors and the women who worked there were not nurses. They had no medical training or knowledge. Their job was simply to provide for their very basic needs—there was no pretense at saving lives. It was not within their ability. Even if it had been, medicine was scarce and for the most part impossible to find.

Because my father was ill and unable to travel, my mother would often go to the hospital to visit his son.

Over time, they had developed a relationship, although my half-brother referred to my mom as his aunt, not his stepmother.

During one particular visit, my mom noticed just how neglected my brother was. His hair was long, dirty, and full of lice. There were white lice on his body. He hadn't been washed or bathed in quite some time. My mom told the nurses that she needed scissors or a knife, something to cut his hair, as well as some water so she could clean him up. Soap and toiletries were just as scarce as medicine, so she did the best she could with a bucket of pond water and a simple rag.

Visitation was only allowed once every ten days. My mom had been making every effort to see him whenever possible. Mom noticed that his health and appearance had deteriorated greatly. Worried about him and realizing the real possibility that he might not survive, she asked him if there was anything he needed. She didn't care what it was, she would find a way to get it to him.

Chicken. He wanted chicken. He told my mom that he had been so hungry for chicken, even if just a couple bites. She listened to him, and although she had no idea how she'd be able to do it, she promised that she would fulfill his wish and bring him chicken on her next visit.

In a land controlled by communist dictators, who also controlled every morsel that went into the people's mouths and the animals and crops, finding and smuggling a chicken into an Angkar-owned hospital was against the law. But my mom was determined. She killed one of the chickens that was being kept for the eggs it laid, and somehow managed to cook and sneak it past the guards and nurses. My mom recalled that my brother was ecstatic. He couldn't believe his eyes when my mom very quietly presented him with what must have been a feast to his eyes. It was obvious that he had been starving, and she was grateful that she had been able to give him this one gift.

She made the trip again, but this time when she visited him, he was delirious. He was crying and screaming in pain and calling for her. Just before her arrival, she was told the nurses had just given him an injection for pain to calm him down. She sat by his bed, where he lay quietly. Then she knew—he was gone. He had passed away in that short period of time after the nurse had given him the shot and my mom's arrival into the room.

At some point in a communist-controlled culture, a person can be deemed to be useless. If you are alive but cannot work or labor for the "Organization," you are considered to be a burden on society. My mom was certain that this had been the case with my half-brother—he was silenced, put out of his misery, eliminated … call it what you will. The fact of the matter was he was no longer of any value to the Regime.

Ever strong, my mom immediately tended to his burial. Knowing that the Angkar would throw his body in a shallow grave where his body could be easily accessed by coyotes and other wild animals, Mom went into action. With the help of some of the hospital workers to carry the dead body of her stepson, she scouted an appropriate grave near the hospital. With a shovel in her hands, she literally dug the grave deep enough to escape the wild carnivore. The process, of course, took hours, and when she was done, she still had to make the long trek home.

My mother was particularly worried about my father, who was also seriously ill. She had notified a friend of my half-brother's death, but urged her not to say a word to my dad. But when my mom arrived home, darkness had already fallen and my father was waiting outside for her. He had been out there for hours, ever since receiving the news of his son's death. This was very painful for my father, and my mom said he was despondent. He cried and cried, wishing he could have been there and could have done something for his son. But without medicine and proper medical treatment, they both knew there was nothing they could have done.

Losing his son was very difficult for my father, and it surely made his health deteriorated even further. At the time, I was no stranger to death, and, in fact, had witnessed people dying. But watching my own father pass away was entirely different and very humbling.

The regime starved everybody—a fact that did not help my father's plight at all. Right after the liberation, we still did not have food. There still were no doctors or medication, which my father desperately needed. My mom went far and wide trying to find remedies to cure his illness. During the Regime, she continued to look for remedies. Even though she went after work on her "own time," she was reprimanded, punished, and reminded that, for workers, there was no such thing as your "own time." She did her best, but her best only served to release him from his pain for a very short time.

While my mom worked to support our family, she asked me to stay by his side and watch him—he was very ill and could not walk. I was too young to do any adult work, so it was up to my mom to do whatever she could to feed us. She was pregnant, too, with my younger brother. Our situation was rather dismal, and I had to help in any way I could.

By this time, my father's entire body was swollen. The top of his feet were round, curved like the back of a turtle. His skin was cracked, and the fluid was seeping out of his skin. Once, he said he was itching and asked me to check his feet. I did, only to find ants crawling in the cracks in his feet, eating the fluid. When I looked to the ground, I noticed that the fluid dripping from his body had created holes in the dirt floor. The holes were smaller than a penny, and each hole had the fluid from his body in it. I watched him in that condition for about four months.

Like my half-brother, my father also requested food before he died. While he was on his deathbed, he wrote a letter to his oldest son, stating that he was craving some of the food that he used to eat and wanted to eat it one more time before he died. He then asked his son to bring him that food, telling him to come quickly. However, his son was living in America at the time and wasn't able to fulfill my dad's last wish.

My father only lived for four months after the liberation. My little brother was only three months old. I knew he didn't want to die. At the time, I didn't really understand death and its permanency, but I knew it was painful. I didn't want to die like that. I didn't want to starve and experience the extreme pain and suffering I'd watched my father endure for months and likely years before he passed away. Witnessing my father suffer has tormented me throughout my life; to this day, it still does.

I now know what had happened to his body. My father had edema, a medical condition caused by fluid retention in the tissues. It was just one of the effects on his body from a lack of nutrition due to starvation. In addition, he also had other disease and illness, and his body simply was not strong enough to fight any of them.

For many years, I was afraid of death because of the pain I'd witnessed. When I was about eight, I truly believed that it was not possible to die without pain. Pain and death were inseparable in my mind—they went hand in hand. In my teenage years, though, I gained a new perspective on death. I am no longer afraid of it or how it will take place. Instead, I choose to focus on living. I've found that being afraid of death causes me to miss out on the present. I also learned that once I die, I won't get a second chance. I only have now—this one opportunity to have this experience and make the best of it. I cannot rewind my life and do it over, living it more fully or better the second time around.

I understand and value being alive very much. There is no magic potion; there is no magic medicine that can cure death. Because of that, we must make the most of the life we are given. Don't hold grudges; don't hold on to angry or negative feelings. Life is a balancing act of past and present. Spend time on the future. Spend time thinking about the past that will enhance the future, but don't over dwell on it. Throw the rest away. Trash it.

I could still be living in fear or grieving the loss of my father. Instead, I want to live and prefer to live in the present. Grounding in the present is being in the moment. It's about implementing S.B.C.I.A. again, "stop, breathe, center, inventory, action," a process I follow whenever I find myself taking my life for granted.

Death is a certainty, and we cannot escape it. But we don't know our expiration date. The one thing we can escape is regret. By living our lives in the moment, we can minimize any regret we may have when our time is up. Take action and seize every day like it was your last. Each day that we are given is a gift. Life is too fragile and unpredictable to waste it worrying about things we cannot control or dwelling on things that we cannot change.

I know I cannot bring my half-brother back; I cannot bring my father back. I can't undo their pain or suffering. But I do know something else—they wanted to live. They didn't want to die—I don't think anyone really does. But nobody wants to live their life like they're dying, either. Our time here is far too precious and unpredictable to take for granted. With so many people fighting for their lives and their health, shouldn't we appreciate them so much more?

Having observed so many people fighting for their health every day, and some literally fighting for their lives, I'll never take my life for granted. Nor will I allow anyone into my life who can dishonor and minimize the gift we call LIFE.

Chapter Nine

**Cruelty Is The Cold Reality**

I'm often asked what it was like to be expected to work as a child. There are some who believe that, surely, our jobs must have been light in nature—the "Organization" officials overseeing us must have given us a little leeway and more than a little slack. After all, we were just kids, right? Well, I knew what I was expected to do, and I didn't for a second test the threat that there would be punishment if I even once crossed the line or refused to follow orders. One day, I learned just how important that was.

All of the young kids had to work, without exception or fail. We had to report to work just as most employed adults do. We were expected to arrive at a specific place by a specific time. Often the "wake up call" and start time was sunrise, being that there was no watch or clock available to use. Being late was not an option, and the sun was usually our reliable time device. We would stay there until we were finished doing whatever tasks and duties were assigned to us that day. We'd finish when the sunset told us it had had enough of its overworked day.

The first rule was that every child had to be at work on time. Now, this is sometimes a challenge for adults—occasionally, they oversleep or find themselves running late. When they do, they usually know the ramifications—their pay is docked, they're given a warning, or if it's habitual and a problem, they might lose their job. Well, losing our job wasn't an option; neither was docking our pay, since we weren't paid. The only thing they could take away from us was one of our daily meals. And I should also point out that we warned before, not after, we did something wrong. We didn't know what the punishment would be if we were late, and nobody wanted to find out.

One day, though, we did. One young skinny boy, who was around six or seven years old at the time, overslept and arrived to work late. Now, he wasn't half an hour, or even an hour late. He arrived just a few minutes past the time we were to report for duty. Because everything and everyone was very closely monitored, there was no way he could sneak in so his late arrival would be unnoticed … or unpunished.

If the intent was to use the boy as an example to the other children, it worked. The punishment for being a few minutes late that was doled out to this boy was beyond cruel and unusual. It was extreme and alarming. While I wish I had never seen it, I know I will never forget it.

The leader of the group grabbed the boy and tied his hands behind his back, leaving him without the ability to defend himself. Then, he stood the child on a nest of fire ants. In America, I have never seen fire ants, but they weren't uncommon in Southeast Asia. We knew that fire ants were to be avoided at all costs by both children and adults alike. Being bit by a fire ant is extremely painful, and the burning sensation caused by their bite and the venom it injects is sheer torture. And this poor boy wasn't being bit by just one fire ant; he was being bit by an entire fire ant farm. Judging by his screams, the experience was excruciating.

But the communist leader wasn't done having his fun. It wasn't enough to put him through such a horrifying and painful experience—he wasn't satisfied yet that the punishment fit the crime. First, he demanded that the boy remain quiet. He was told not to cry or scream, and if he dared to do so, he would make things even worse. I watched as the tears streamed down the boy's face. I hoped and prayed he wouldn't scream or cry, but he couldn't stop. The sting of hundreds of fire ants was too much for him to bear. Even at my age, it was apparent that he was in sheer agony. I didn't think they could do anything to him that could hurt him anymore than already had. But I was wrong. Leaving the boy standing on the nest of fire ants, where he continued to be bit repeatedly, the leader pursued to the second phase of his punishment. He whipped the boy, lashing at him over and over and over.

Knowing how painful this was to watch, I can't even begin to imagine the depth and extent of the pain they made the boy endure, not once, but twice—maybe more, in truth, I lost count. The leader pulled out his whip and administered a second and then third set of beatings before he was fully satisfied that the boy, who by now was barely conscious, had learned his lesson. It seemed like an eternity before it finally stopped.

Watching him, I felt very sad. For one thing, the boy was about my age at the time. My heart ached for that young defenseless boy, and I couldn't believe that such a depth of cruelty could actually exist in someone's heart. And it was toward a child. He was just a little boy, and believe me, nothing he could have done, *nothing*, could have justified the treatment he received that day.

Not only was I sad, but I was also frightened to the core. Witnessing that punishment left me extremely nervous that I would make one wrong move or be one second late, and I vowed to never allow that to happen. I had never been late to work before, but from that moment on, I made sure I didn't take any chances. Like a child who wanted to play, I got to work early, before anybody else arrived, but I wasn't eagerly reporting for work … I was saving myself from suffering a similar fate as that little boy.

I wish I had never witnessed that incident and the excruciating terror and pain that I heard in that bony boy's screams and that I could erase what I saw in his eyes and the tears that poured out of them. As strong as it stands, it haunts me; and I still hurt for him to this day because of that recollection. I simply cannot figure out how anyone—a communist leader, a parent, *anyone*—could treat a child with such a mean and vengeful heart. There was no mercy, no compassion, either for his age or his size. To me, the person who deliberately hurt this child had no feelings whatsoever. His heart was hardened, cold, and so very cruel.

As an adult, I still cannot fathom such cruelty, particularly toward a small and defenseless child. I just do not understand such behavior, or the conscience, or lack of it, that would allow it to occur. However, it happens still to this day. We don't live in a communist-controlled country, and children aren't expected, or legally allowed, to work at such a young age. If they did, they certainly wouldn't be subjected to such treatment. Nonetheless, small defenseless children are brutally harmed every day. We read about it in the newspapers and see it on the news.

Maybe it shocks and touches me so deeply because I was unfortunate to have witnessed it and felt the long-term effects and fear from the pain that was inflicted upon a young boy. Maybe it's because I've always had a compassionate heart and am troubled when I see a person suffering. But I know now that I don't have to sit silently and allow it to happen. I am no longer powerless. Instead, I can use my voice, my story, and my experiences to bring some much-needed attention to tragedies like these and hope that, in some way, it will make a difference, not only for children, but for all people who are victims of physical, mental, or emotional cruelty.

The lesson that I was intended to learn years ago was that I should never, ever be late for work. However, the lasting lesson and impression that was left and embedded in my soul was entirely different. That is, there is no cause, political or otherwise, or no error great and grave enough that any human being should harm another. Pain and injury are problems in our society, just as they were in Cambodia decades ago. Because they are an ongoing problem and one that victimizes those who are weakest, they cannot also be the solution to *any* problem whatsoever.

The only real solution is love and compassion. There is more power in a kind and loving touch than there is in an angry fist. Those who are abused desperately need that love and compassion. Those who are abusive need it even more—they've grown cold and have allowed power and greed to harden their hearts. I believe that our hearts are meant to feel—to love—not to sting like the thousand fire ants on that poor unfortunate boy. Perhaps if we spent more time focusing on compassion, kindness and forgiveness, there would be far fewer defenseless victims in the wake we leave behind. I can attest to the fact that the damage caused by cruelty lasts much, much longer than the physical scars that it leaves behind. Yet we can overcome these emotional scars. I believe that in large part I have conquered many of these lingering beasts. Not all, I'm sure. Life is a process, and I'm not done.

Here's some of what I've learned about this process from my mentors. One of the medical assessment tests for cardiac health is the stress test. They put us on a staircase or treadmill and bring our heart rate up to a very high point, then reduce the stress and measure how long it takes to 'recover' to our normal state. Well, I've learned that there's another recovery rate that is important to measure health. It's the emotional recovery rate, and it's measured by how long it takes for us to get from peak negative emotional states down to our normal state of peace and calm. Some never come down and you can easily identify them. They hold on to their negative stories and emotions like they are their badge of honor. They play the P.L. U.M. game; Poor Little Unfortunate Me. And they play the A.I.A. game: Ain't It Awful. Imagine if they had a strategy to forgive and move on? I believe that they would live years longer.

My question to you is this: What insult or injury has been done to you that you have forgiven in a way that it no longer holds a negative emotional charge? Do you know how you came to forgive? If you do, then that might be your strategy to forgive others quickly; your strategy to move from poor little unfortunate me into, 'I easily and freely release these negative emotions and selfishly forgive completely.' Take a moment and jot that strategy down if you are aware of it. If not, you may want to give it some consideration because you somehow found it in yourself to forgive and it will serve you well if you can move from 'unconscious competent' to 'conscious competent.' There's gold in that strategy. See if you can identify it and reuse it where necessary.

My next question is this: What insult or injury has been done to you that you have NOT forgiven?

Perhaps you would benefit by applying your strategy to get past that and move into that awesome state of peaceful forgiveness. Sometimes it's not so easy, but you know at your core that it's totally worth the effort. Just sayin'.

Chapter Ten

## Weighing Decisions

Compassion has always been deeply ingrained in me, so much that it is one of the defining posts of my life. Like my nationality and the color of my skin, I cannot separate myself from it, even if I wanted to … and I don't. I truly try to exercise compassion and kindness with all people I meet. It's a habit that began long ago, when I was just a child.

After my father's death and our country's liberation from the Khmer Rouge Regime, Cambodia was still a land of turmoil and unrest. I was living at home with my grandmother, mother, and little brother, but my mom needed to fulfill one of her greatest wishes—making sure her children received a formal education. Because she had been a servant as a child, it was a luxury that had never been afforded her, and her lack of schooling had always made her feel inferior. She wanted more for her kids, and giving us an education became one of her highest priorities. To make it happen, my mother sent me to live with a family friend in a city away from the village. I'm not sure how she did it because we barely had any possessions, but somehow she managed to send me to school and give me a small amount of money just in case I needed food or supplies.

I managed to save some of that money so I could buy something for my younger brother to give him when I came home for my visits. One time, I bought a whole stick of sugar cane—the whole thing, which stretched about seven feet from end to end. Not only did I buy the whole sugar cane, but I intentionally searched for the biggest and longest one I could find to bring home.

But carrying it was a struggle. I never realized how heavy a stalk of sugarcane really is until I attempted to walk home with it. I tried to drag it, which didn't work because it was awkward and slowed me down, making me arrive home far too late. The only way I could transport it was to carry it on my shoulder. The weight would slow me down so much; I had to stop and take frequent breaks to rest, which would make me arrive even later. The walk was four to five hours from the village, and that was without taking frequent breaks. I didn't want to pay someone to taxi me because that would cost extra money, which I didn't have. To me, any extra money was better spent on my brother.

My brother had been waiting for me when I finally arrived. Excited to see the sugar cane, he asked my mom to cut it into pieces, block by block, and he counted how many pieces he had. Savoring it, he ate only one piece a day, keeping track of how many days the sugar cane would last.

The difficulties in getting sugar cane made me rethink my strategy. Knowing how ecstatic and happy my brother had been when he saw his gift, I knew I wanted to bring him something special the next time. But I also knew it would not be sugar cane. It was simply far too difficult to trudge home with a seven-foot stalk of sugar.

So I thought a watermelon would be a good idea. After all, it wasn't seven foot long. But I quickly learned it was heavy. Because I was small, it took both arms to carry the watermelon, and just like with the sugar cane, I found myself making frequent stops to rest. The more I rested, the longer it took me to get home. It took even longer to get home that day.

As I got closer to home, I saw a tiny figure in the distance. At first, I couldn't make out what it was—to me, it resembled a small dot in a rice field. Then, it occurred to me. It was him. Then I thought, no, it couldn't possibly be my little brother. There was no way he had walked that far. But sure enough, as he got closer, I could see I was right. It was my brother, my little brother who I loved so much, and he was too far from home. Wearing a red shirt that was riding up on his stomach but wearing no pants, he looked like Winnie the Pooh, except I could see how sad he looked. He broke my heart when he saw me and greeted me with a cry, "What took you so long?"

Obviously, he had been waiting for quite some time, and maybe longer since it had taken me so long to arrive.

The look on his face totally changed when he saw the watermelon I'd bought and carried all the way from the city just for him. I wanted to make him happy, and if looks could talk, I didn't disappoint. Seeing the look on his face, the watermelon was well worth the wait. To me, the joy I knew I brought my brother that day made it well worth the difficulty I experienced getting it home. The happiness in his bright and beautiful smile just lit up his entire face.

It warmed my heart to do something nice for my brother. I knew that he had never experienced anything good while living in the village. We were so poor, and my father had passed away so he didn't have a male figure in his life. He never had treats or special treatment. I so very much wanted to give him a few of those happy moments and something to look forward to. Every time I came home, it was like Christmas for him—it didn't matter what I brought for him. The only thing that mattered was that I remembered him.

I understood what my brother was going through. After all, I had experienced a life of scarcity, as well. I was still a child myself and didn't have anything, but his happiness was one of my top priorities, just as my mom's desire to educate her children was one of hers.

I learned that, while it's not always easy and can sometimes be very difficult, it was the feeling that I got when I saw the joy in him that was most important. When it became a heavy burden, I'd focus on my end goal and the joy I just knew I would see on his face. That's what kept me going and made it worth it.

Sure, it was more than a little difficult to accomplish my feat, but when I kept my focus on my brother and the happiness I was bringing to him, the discomfort and pain would evaporate enough to keep me going. The only way to do it was to focus on my objective, not the obstacles and challenges along the way.

You don't have to be a child living in Cambodia, carrying sugar cane or watermelon for hours, to understand this concept. Everyone has difficulties and times when they feel like they cannot go any farther. Whether it's too painful or there are just too many obstacles in the way, they take their eye off their goal. Believe me, obstacles are the only things people will see when they take their eyes off their goals.

As humans, we can really only focus on one thing at a time. I learned this as a child. Staring at two stars in the sky, if I removed my focus from one, I'd find that I'd lose sight of the other—it would totally disappear from my field of vision. As a result, the mind becomes limited, only able to see what is before it at that precise moment. However, when I focus on both stars, they are both visible at all times—I'm able to see the bigger and whole picture. For me at the time, the end goal and the joy which I was able to bring to my brother's life helped me forget about the obstacles. If I'd focused on only one star, I would have only seen the obstacles, and they would have made it even more difficult and painful for me to achieve my goal.

Remember, hardships and difficulties are temporary. However, joy stays with you for life, especially when you spread it to the people you care about. Sometimes we'll go to the most extreme measures just to know we made a difference in the life of the people who are important to us. I know I'd do it again just to see him smile, even if it means walking for hours carrying a long cane of sugar or a heavy round watermelon. Indeed, when it comes to spreading a little happiness, the reward is far greater than the effort.

## Chapter Eleven

### Expect The Best, Prepare For The Worst

It was 1979 when the Vietnamese soldiers invaded Cambodia, overthrew the Khmer Rouge Regime, and liberated our country. However, that didn't put an end to our plight. Cambodians were very poor; they had lost their homes, their possessions, and their jobs. The Vietnamese invasion liberated us from the oppression and starvation inflicted upon us by the Regime; however, our country was still under Communist rule. The future held more of the same with no end in sight. In essence, our government had changed, but the country was still consumed by massive and underlining fear and the possibility that the Khmer Rouge Regime would return.

Before my father died, he wrote a letter to his oldest son, asking him to take to take us to America, where my dad believed we would have a better life, one where we wouldn't be forced to live in poverty, where opportunities existed, and people were free from government brutality. My father never lived to see his response.

In that letter, his oldest son agreed to help us and told us to find a way to get to American as soon as we could. Not knowing what to do, my mother agreed to take the risk, and in January, 1984, we began our journey to America, leaving behind the only country and people we had ever known.

No one traveled with us; it was just my mom, my little brother and I. Mom didn't know what to do and could only follow what little advice she received along the way. We left home with very little money and fewer possessions, because we didn't have much of either and traveling with our baggage and belongings would only draw attention to the fact that our trip was intended to be a long, even permanent, one.

Some might call it a journey, but in reality, in order to get to America, we had to first escape Cambodia. In order to do that, we had to get past soldiers from three parties—the Vietnamese Communist soldiers, and the remaining soldiers from the Khmer Rouge Regime, and a new party whose claim was to liberate the country from the Vietnamese-controlled regime. No one could suspect that we were attempting to escape. If we were caught trying to escape the country, the punishment would be very severe. My mom was told those who were caught could be killed, and/or tied up and drowned.

Because the probability was higher of death, we traveled with very few possessions and with the utmost secrecy. Our lives were literally on the line.

The destination of the first trek of our escape was a refugee camp in Thailand. The day we left our village, my mom told me we had to take a train. At the time, it was the only form of transportation that was both available and affordable. This particular train was packed; people were packed into every available spot. Some people even strung hammocks so they could sleep above the floor. We didn't have a hammock, though, and were stuck sleeping on the floor, which was beyond filthy. The three of us stayed together on the nasty floor, where we were joined by chickens, bugs, urine from animals, and an unbelievable amount of unidentifiable filth.

The trip to Phnom Penh, the capital city, took us an entire day, a day which my mom spent in sorrow and sadness. She was leaving her home and family and everything she had ever known, putting herself and her family at great risk without knowing our future. She wanted a better life and to fulfill my father's wishes, but she didn't want to leave everything she knew and those she loved behind. We were going to America for one reason—because we were told to. The fact that I was sick didn't make matters any better. I wasn't a good traveler and suffered from motion sickness very frequently.

As a child, I was quite experienced in the field of transportation because we moved across the country by train, boats, pedicab, motorcycles, bicycle taxis, and my own two calloused and sometimes blistered feet. Among travelers, there were many others who were also attempting to escape the country. Of course, they noticed that my mother was traveling alone, with two small children, and it was obvious that crossing the border without assistance would be nearly impossible.

It quickly became evident that our family stood out, which would put us in danger. My mom had very dark skin, and my brother and I had light skin. Picture a crow and two doves—that is what our family looked like. In order to pretend that we weren't traveling with our mom, because no one would believe we were her children, a scheme was devised. My brother and I were separated from each other and our mother. I had to go with one family and pretend to be their daughter, and my brother had to travel with another family as their son. Our mother would follow behind at a distance so the authorities would not suspect that we were escaping the country together.

My mom traveled on the road on a taxi motorcycle until she neared the first checkpoint and had to stop and await her turn. Suddenly, she saw me and my little brother sitting alone on the side of the road, clinging to each other and crying hysterically. We were scared and alone, without any supervision. My mom told me that her heart fell to the ground and she was devastated. The people who were supposed to be our surrogate parents had abandoned us, leaving us entirely alone and on our own. Mom later told me that somebody knew we were escaping the country, and the people who were charged with us had been caught and reported to the authorities. They were able to go on, but only after they bribed the soldiers and did not to take us with them. The families who were charged with our transportation and safety didn't want to take that risk.

It seemed like my mom had extraordinary challenges. Reunited, my mom swooped us up and took us with her; all three of us piled onto her taxi motorcycle and made the trip together. The accommodations were rough at best and having two children with her on the motorcycle certainly made our escape more difficult and more dangerous, but it was our only choice.

From that experience, I learned so much about loyalty. People can make promises, but if it can jeopardize or endanger their lives or circumstances, they will abandon you, especially if they are not family. When push comes to shove, they will look out for themselves first and foremost. Only true family and true friends will be loyal and willing to risk their safety or circumstances to stand by us.

In any challenges, I know that I cannot rely on just anyone—I must be ready and be prepared to face my challenges on my own and cannot depend on others, even if their promise seems sincere. Although it wasn't safe, my mother never deserted me and my brother. In fact, she was the one and only person we could rely on. She was the only person she had to rely on—the assistance that had been promised to her had abandoned ship at the first sign of difficulty.

It is not so much about trust as it is about knowing—there are just too many variables and factors that can influence others, and it is our natural instinct to protect ourselves and those who belong to us. For that reason, it is not wise, especially in matters of life and death or situations where the outcome is critical, to leave our fate in the hands of strangers and those who have no stake in our safety or wellbeing.

Trust is not something that should be given lightly. It takes years to build, but only seconds to destroy. I've heard it said that trust is not based on its bind, or the simple fact that someone is available and in your life, but real dependable trust is instead based on its bond—the deeper the connection, the more loyal the trust. It reminds me of a story I once heard about a little girl and her father. They were crossing a bridge, and the father asked his daughter to hold his hand so she wouldn't fall into the river below. The little girl refused, saying, "No, you hold my hand instead." The father was puzzled by her response and asked her what the difference was. With maturity beyond her years, the little girl explained. "Well, if I hold your hand, there is a chance that I might let it go. But, Dad, if you hold, I know that you will never, ever let it go."

What a wise little girl. Even children, like I was as we were traveling to the border of Thailand, know that if there is one thing they can count on, it's their family. Anyone else simply doesn't have the bond necessary to stay with us when times get tough.

In the final analysis, I've learned that this is my life, and I'm responsible for it. The only one in charge of it is me and a greater spirit. I cannot delegate that responsibility to others or place the outcome of it in anyone else's hands. They might let go. The only thing I can do is expect the best, while also preparing for the worst. Then, I can be assured that my fate doesn't rest in the wrong people—those who have conflicting motives or who lack the connection or bond, emotional, familial, or otherwise, to stay by my side when the going gets rough.

"Sometimes the threat is not those that oppose you, it's those who were supposed to be beside you." - Anonymous

## Chapter Twelve

### Flex Or Die

While I strive to avoid the political aspect of my youth, it was a defining factor in almost everything we did and the decisions my mother had to make. The truth is the political environment in Cambodia was disturbed at the time. Of course, I was too young to understand the complexities of politics at the time, but I've since expanded my knowledge of Cambodia's political environment in an effort to truly grasp the country's turmoil and the danger our family faced, even after Cambodia was liberated from the Khmer Rouge Regime. Unlike democracies, where people elect governments, our country was divided, with several governments fighting to win control. The upheaval could be likened to a civil war between numerous parties. The Khmer Rouge Regime was hiding in multiple camps in the jungle bordering Thailand. There was still yet another party that claimed it would liberate Cambodia from Communism altogether.

This political environment posed great danger for Cambodians, especially those who sought refuge. Anyone attempting to escape was at risk. No party wanted Cambodians to leave the country or to join with the independents. Therefore, they maintained an iron-tight control over the borders and were extremely suspicious of anyone who might be attempting to escape the country. Even the mere suspicion of attempting to escape was considered a criminal act.

This was the political climate my mother was trying to escape. Traveling alone with two small children, she had few resources to guide her and had to rely on her instincts for survival. She listened to other travelers as they warned of potential dangers and counted on faith each step of the way, knowing that the danger lurked at every turn.

Thinking we had almost made it, we arrived at the final checkpoint, where once again it became evident that traveling with her children placed my mother in extreme suspicion. As we anticipated at the beginning of our journey, the soldier who stopped us noticed that our mother's skin was much darker than ours, which made him believe that we were not her natural children. Instead, he was convinced that my mom was smuggling Chinese children across the border, and being paid to do so.

All my mother had to go on was the truth, and a wing and a prayer. The soldier interrogated her relentlessly, then turning to my brother, who was only four years old at the time, thinking he could get him to talk and expose the "truth." He asked my brother, "Is this your mom? That is not your mom, right?" hoping that he'd get my brother to spill the beans. Back and forth and back and forth he went, from my brother to my mom and my mom to my brother. With every question and insinuation, he was met with the same answers—my mom insisted that my brother was, indeed, her son, and my brother wouldn't budge as the soldier tried to get him to admit otherwise. Still, the soldier refused to believe them.

They held us, refusing to let us go. After a while, they gave us some water to quench our thirst, but we were so very hungry and they wouldn't give us anything to eat. By this time, my little brother was not only hungry, he was also irritated and very hot. Those circumstances don't bode well with an unpredictable, frightened little boy, and I think it's safe to say that we were all surprised when my brother picked up a piece of wood that had come from a broken wagon wheel and smacked that soldier square on the head. Bam!

If my mom had been anxious for our safety before, you can imagine the depths of her fear when my brother struck the soldier. My mom said soldier became so angry that his face turned as red as a tomato. At that point, she was certain that all three of us had met our fate and were going to die. After all, not only were we trying to escape the country, but it was also suspected that my mom was smuggling Chinese children—add physically attacking the soldier to our list of crimes, and we were doomed.

Mom resorted to the only thing she could think of—begging for forgiveness. I can recall her talking so fast, telling the soldier to please not be mad, that he was just a little kid, he didn't mean it, he didn't know better. Panicked and pleading, she knew we were at the mercy of the soldier, if he had any mercy at all.

Whether it's success or survival one is striving for, sometimes you have to resort to unlikely resources. Luckily, my mom had one—she knew how to speak a little Vietnamese. Able to communicate with the soldier, even just a little, gave her an advantage, albeit a small one, but she needed every resource she could get at that time. With some level of communication and understanding between Mom and the soldier, she felt she could try to relate to him and use a little power of persuasion.

Just as she was attempting to do that, she heard another soldier yelling to the soldier who was confronting us. "Are you taking the bribe alone? You have to share it with me." Those words gave her a glimmer of hope that our plight was not entirely doomed. Realizing that the soldiers were open to taking bribes, she took some of the very little money she had left and placed it under one of his feet. Then she acted like she hadn't done anything and continued to beg him to let us go. She repeated for the umpteenth time that we were not armed and that my brother really was her son.

Then, miraculously, another thing happened that finally did the trick. By this time, my brother was extremely hungry, and my mom had no choice but to feed him—breastfeed him, that is. Worn down from my mother's pleading and my brother's crying, the soldier couldn't argue after witnessing my mom breastfeed, and he reluctantly accepted the fact that they were mother and son. Pretending like nothing had transpired, he sent us on our way. He never once looked down or acknowledged the money (which you can be certain he took after we left), but he did offer a piece of advice, telling my mom to stay off the main road and take the small road, instead.

Immensely grateful, Mom didn't overstay her welcome, but stopped just long enough to ask the soldier where she could find the small road. After telling her where she could find it, he also told her who to ask for when she got there.

We had escaped again. We had another chance for freedom—another chance to live! Relieved beyond measure, we knew that our release had not only been unlikely, but that it was also too close for comfort. If it hadn't been for a couple small factors, we might have been imprisoned or killed that day.

I certainly hope that I never relive that experience or teeter so closely to danger again in my lifetime. I'm well aware that our outcome could have been far different. I shudder to think what would have happened if my mom hadn't known another language, if we hadn't had any money at all, or if my brother hadn't been ravenously hungry at the time.

Initially, my mom didn't think she had any resources that could have saved us, but in fact, when push came to shove, her survival instincts were able to reveal resources that she didn't know existed. I believe it was divine intervention or even fate that spared us that day, but I also know that without faith, our outcomes might have been very different. My mother never gave up, and she never gave up hope—two factors that played very big roles in our release.

While it's highly unlikely that I will ever face soldiers at a checkpoint ever again in my life, there will always be situations that call for innovative thinking. There are always times when we're seeking a solution that we already have what we need, but we don't know it yet. If we get caught up and lost in the severity of our situation, we might lose our ability to maintain our composure long enough to find the answers.

From that lesson, I realized that knowing another language or learning a new skill can be a plus. Mom is street smart. Sure, there may be times when we don't feel that the knowledge is useful, but we never really know what the future holds in store. There may come a time when even the smallest bit of knowledge or the most unlikely skill can be the turning point in any situation. In order to benefit from it, though, we should always remain vigilant and observant. There are resources available to us if we open up our peripheral vision so we can see beyond what is immediately in front of us. By staying alert, we are able to identify those resources and use them in surprising ways.

This checkpoint gave me a valuable lesson. It was a wake-up call, in fact, that enlightened me tremendously. Because of this experience, I know firsthand that nothing is ever certain. There is always a way, somewhere, somehow, to achieve a different result than the one that is threatening to occur. And we already have many things we need to make it happen—as long as we're able to keep our eyes and minds open enough to allow them to expose themselves to us.

## Chapter Thirteen

### Life In A Refugee Camp

Have you ever been anxious to get somewhere, only to find that when you arrived, you really didn't want to be "there," either? Maybe you were in a hurry to grow up, but then found that adult life wasn't as fun as you had imagined. Or maybe you couldn't wait until the day you graduated from college and got that dream job, but when you did, it fell far short of your expectations. There are so many things we wait for, but when the time finally comes, we find that we're somewhat disappointed with the reality.

We see it every day on the freeway. People are in a rush to get somewhere, but when they arrive to their destination, they can't wait to be somewhere else. That was me when we arrived at the refugee camp. We had but one goal—to arrive to the refugee camp safely. Of course, we were anxious to get there, and we longed for the protection that the camp offered. But that didn't mean I had to like it. And I didn't. We had risked our lives to get there, but I knew almost immediately that I couldn't wait to leave.

Khao I Dang was the name of the refugee camp, but everyone referred to it by its acronym, KID. Let me tell you, though, this was a far cry from a kid camp and the fun one would anticipate having there. First of all, the camp was surrounded by fencing—two layers of barbed wire. Its menacing presence wasn't much of a welcome mat.

The camp sat at the foot of a very lush green mountain. Its scenic view was one of the only things of beauty the camp had to offer. I'd often sit and stare at it from a distance, longing to explore it, but settling for admiring it, for the barbed wire kept me from getting any closer to it. We couldn't cross that barbed wire or attempt to leave the camp—those who longed to do so knew that on the other side of that barbed wire lurked the very real threat of being shot.

Because the barbed wire marked the boundary of the camp, people didn't want to live in huts close to the fence because it was dangerous. Again, the fence could keep people out, but it was no match for a bullet. Everyone learned very quickly that the safest place to be was away from the fences. The fact of the matter is that most people who managed to seek refuge in the camp didn't want to leave—they had risked their life and limb to get there, and it offered their only hope of escaping the oppression Cambodians faced at that time.

The camp was 2.3 square kilometers. Later, I researched the camp and found claims that at its peak, more than 300,000 lived in the camp ... at the same time. I won't argue that fact. I remember there were so many people—more people than I'd ever seen gathered together in one location in my entire life. People were everywhere, seemingly shoulder to shoulder. Even the huts were occupied by two families, one living on each side. As soon as one family would leave, another one would move in.

Our hut, like all of the rest, was very small. It consisted of one bed made of bamboo, which was shared among the three of us, and a tiny area that held what could be called a miniature stove, but it was not a stove in any conventional respect. It was merely three rocks strategically placed together so that you could balance a pot above and the wood fire below.

We had to rely on the camp for all of our needs. Food, especially water, had to be brought in daily. Everybody received four gallons of water for eating, drinking, and bathing. If you were late picking up your rations, you'd get no water for the day. People who lived there were legal and had a ration card, which they had to present in order to receive their daily or weekly allotments. Even our firewood was distributed to us in limited quantities. Along with other supplies and necessities, we received our quota on a weekly and sometimes biweekly basis. Like most of our food and supplies, the allotment didn't fill the need. When people ran out of food or other items, they had to find a way to self-support their families. Some families traded money or jewels for the food they needed to survive, and some were lucky enough to have relatives outside the camp who sent them money from time to time. We were among them, in as much as my oldest half-brother and his family were generous enough to send us money to fund our escape to freedom.

Most of the time, we had no money. We had to settle for what was given to us, and if we wanted to survive, we had to find a way to make it last. My mom told me just how little we lived on—every other week, we'd receive two grams of chicken and two grams (.07 ounce) of pork per person. Once a week, we'd get two cans of tuna and fresh vegetables. Because the meat was barely enough to last for only one week, I can remember many times when the only thing we had to eat was rice.

To me, while it's not the hell that I used to experience under the direct control of the Pol Pot, the refugee camps were their own sort of hell on earth. I've too many bad (understatement) memories. I simply didn't want to remember them. Maybe that's why many of the day-to-day and minute-to-minute experiences I had while I was there have escaped my memory. My hard drive must had reached its maximum capacity and automatically deleted them to make room for greater and happier things to come in my life—one of which is it gives me the courage to write this very book you're reading now.

I simply couldn't fathom why so many people had such an intense desire to be there, so much so that they would risk their lives to and leave behind everything they ever knew just to get there. After all, KID camp was no picnic. Of course, there was the vision and hope of something better. The refugee camp symbolized something far greater than its environment. It was the door to a better life. Once there, refugees knew they were safe from the adversaries, and there was also the possibility that one day they would be able to leave the camp without fear or repercussions.

As it was, though, the camp wasn't much different than living under the Regime. Food was scarce, and we were still hungry. We still didn't have our own home or any furnishings or possessions. There were still rules, quite a few, actually, and we were expected to follow them. You learn very quickly what you need to do to survive in such circumstances. And let's not forget, we weren't living at the Hilton. We were sharing a tiny hut with another family, eating the bare minimum to survive, and were packed together like sardines. While we had fled communist rule, we were totally dependent on the camp for survival.

Yet, hundreds and hundreds of thousands of people couldn't wait to get there. But it wasn't the camp itself that they longed for, it was what it represented. To us, it represented freedom. While I loathed every minute of living at KID camp, I was old enough to know that this was where we needed to be … for now. I also knew, though, that if I was going to move on to our life's next destination, I would have to set aside my impatience and learn how to be patient and accept our situation. It was mentally challenging, but I had to believe that good things come to people who wait. I was old enough to understand that I needed to reach deeply and find the faith that this, too, would pass and we would be eventually receive our long-awaited reward.

Bettering myself required optimism that I didn't know I had. I couldn't chance the depression that would certainly overtake me if I for one minute didn't have the hope that our situation was temporary. I remind myself of that whenever I find that I'm not happy with the status quo. It doesn't matter if the situation involves finances or a job, the mindset needs to be the same. First, I have to truly believe that I am where I am at the present moment for a reason. Then, I remind myself that my situation is temporary. And most important, I accept the full responsibility for changing it.

Nothing in life is permanent. People come and go, jobs come and go, and money flows out as fast as it comes in. Every experience in our life is just one stop toward our ultimate destination. When it's occurring, we need to make the best of it and use that experience to prepare ourselves for what lies ahead. In this case, we might have been in a hurry to get to KID camp, and I was certainly in a hurry to leave it … but if the rest our journey was going to be successful, we had to be patient.

I had to remind myself of that often as I gazed longingly at that big green mountain in the distance. Like the rest of the world scrambling to get from one place to another, my desire to leave tested my patience for three and a half years. I had nothing to rely on but hope and faith that the barbed wire that kept us safe for the time being would eventually set us free.

All KID camp pictures are courtesy of **Jack Dunford**. Jack, I thank you and appreciate the precious pictures you shared to the public. I'm sure others appreciate you as well.

*Photo 1: KID camp July 1986. There was another layer of barbed wire that I remembered we had to cross into the camp.*

*Photo 2: KID camp June 1985, people were getting their ration.*

*Photo 4: KID camp 1980s, people were getting water.*

*Photo 3: KID Camp 1980s, people were getting one bucket of water (about 4 gallons or 15 liters) per person.*

*Picture 5: KID camp 1990, Main Gate*

Chapter Fourteen

## KID Camp: Robbery At Night

The KID camp was located in Thailand. Initially, it was a designed as a humanitarian effort to aid the hundreds of thousands of refugees fleeing from Cambodia. On November 21, 1979, the first day it opened, 4,800 refugees entered the camp. Its open door policy enticed the arrival of many more people, and more than 1,800 people entered the camp daily. With such a huge influx of arrivals, Thailand closed KID's open door policy on January 24, 1980, just two months after the camp had opened. It was administered by the Thai Ministry of the Interior, the Thai army and the United Nations High Commissioner for Refugees (UNHCR).

However, it didn't take long before refugees sought illegal entry into the camp, which introduced an element of theft and violence into the already cramped and difficult living quarters. Given that the majority of the refugees had very little in the way of money or personal possessions and the fact that most were totally dependent on the UNHCR government for food and survival, the illegals only served to make an already volatile environment even more dangerous. Such was the climate when we moved into the camp in 1984.

I remember being awakened many nights by alerts of robberies being conducted from people outside the camp. Who they were, we never really knew because they were very good at what they did; they robbed and stole in the dark of night. When we were in our deepest sleep, they'd come into the camp. People would begin yelling, "Robbers are coming—run!" We'd grab our belongings and run toward the main gate, which used by the outside workers who came in during the day to work. Those workers always left before dark, however, because the camp was not secure. The main gate, though, was considered to be secure, so it was our "base" during robberies.

To get to the main gate, we had to run across a sewage creek, and if it was monsoon season, we'd run through the pouring rain to safety. Naturally, many of us were not prepared to be seen in public, and many were in various stages of dress. As you can imagine, this was a source of embarrassment for some of the men who would flee their huts wearing only their underwear, especially since the area we ran to was one of the few places that had electricity at night.

Crime caused many sleepless nights for the refugees. Even when we were sleeping, we were on guard, always listening, always watching for any sign of danger lurking outside the fence or in.

To show that we were, in fact, legal refugees, we were given ration cards and had to wear an ID at all times. Forgetting it or losing it would result in being beaten, being deported, or both. The card was quite big, so much that it made the refugees feel like prisoners. In truth, in many ways we were.

Thai soldiers routinely came into the camp and conducted random checks for illegal refugees. When they were spotted, warnings were sent out so those without ration cards and IDs could hide and not be caught. It was dangerous, but the illegal refugees stayed in the hopes that they would eventually be given a card of their own. They were willing to take the risk, but often escaped being found, thanks to the heads up given by the other refugees.

The soldiers usually came in during the day, but occasionally conducted a surprise inspection at night. One particular night stands out in my mind. A man lived two huts away from us, and when the soldiers arrived, they began beating him. I could hear the kicking and the hitting, but I will never forget the sounds of the man's moans and screams. This went on for quite a while—during that time, everyone around remained silent. No one, not one person, stepped up to aid him or attempt to put a stop to the brutality. It was as if nothing was happening.

In reality, no one could have stopped the soldiers. Attempting to would jeopardize their own safety and wellbeing. Because the UNHCR was not on site at night, the soldiers had the power to do whatever they wanted, whether it was illegal according to international standards of human rights or not. Not facing any repercussions, the soldiers were free to inflict pain and punishment on anyone if they knew that the UNCHR were not around to see.

The next day, I saw the man and the evidence the beating had left behind. Clutching his stomach tightly, he was unable to sit up straight. His eyes were red and bruises marked his face. He had been kicked by the soldiers' boots and struck repeatedly with the butt of their guns. He told us that they used the electric wires in his hut to beat him, as well.

Why? What did this man do to justify such a beating? Well, there was a curfew in the camp, and every night at a certain time the electricity would be turned off in the main grid. The only electricity would be in the main streets as darkness befell the huts. However, this man had been an electrician and he used his own resources and skill to install electricity in his own hut. Whether the rules were right or wrong, fair or unfair, for what they were, he broke them. But they certainly didn't have to break him. They beat him mercilessly.

He never reported his beating, undoubtedly, because he was afraid. There was a real fear that he would be punished for doing so. He had already experienced the consequences of upsetting the soldiers and certainly didn't want to anger them again. It was a damned if you do and damned if you don't scenario.

I was told that the man coughed up blood for a few months after the beating. Then my family was moved to the next camp. To this day, I don't think he survived to see his young son grow up. From this experience, I learned that some people have the capacity to be beyond cruel. Even animals don't inflict that sort of pain on other animals for mere pleasure. But these soldiers certainly did. Instead of simply asking him to turn off his electricity and penalizing him in a more reasonable way, they chose a violent path. In that path, they created physical injury, probably murder, and certainly long-lasting emotional trauma.

Let me be clear that I do not judge or hold bias against the whole race or nationality just because of some bad people. It leaves me with a deep desire to live and promote peace in every way that I can. I cannot fathom a situation where a person does not show compassion for his fellow man. As a result of these childhood experiences, if I was alone with another person in the middle of the desert, I would, without hesitation, share my food or water with him or her, even if it meant sacrifice. I know that we all want to live, prosper, and be happy. Violence or abuse toward one another can only move us further away from those goals. In my life, I've seen far too much violence. We all have, whether on TV, in movies, or in person. Violence is a choice. Peace is a choice. Compassion is a choice. Choose well.

My takeaway from these experiences is that conflicts can be approached and settled without violence or cruelty. Questions can be asked and kind request can be made. People are more apt to respond favorably to a gentle word than a hard fist. There can be cooperation in this world, without the need to force submission on others. By sharing such atrocities against humanity, it is my hope that people will become aware of the effects of their actions and choose a gentler, kinder path. Given the choice, isn't it easier to support each other, rather destroy each other?

## Chapter Fifteen

### Culture Shock

Since living in the camp was often scary, it might come as a surprise that leaving the camp was in some ways even scarier. Going forth into the great unknown was frightening. When it was time for us to leave the camp and continue on to our destination, I had butterflies in my stomach—huge butterflies that wouldn't go away.

It was early in the morning when we left the camp. Wearing my best clothes, I sat on the bus with my brother and mother. Knowing that we were leaving could have been cause for celebration, but it made me extremely nervous. The bus was supposed to carry us to camp number three, which would be our final destination before traveling to the United States. So many thoughts and possibilities crossed my mind. Maybe the bus would break down or something would go wrong and we'd end up back at KID camp. So many fears raced through my mind before the bus started driving away. It wasn't until the camp was far in the distance that I allowed myself to believe, even for a short second, that we were actually going where we were supposed to.

Sitting on that bus, I made a commitment to myself that I would make a better life for myself and my family after everything I'd gone through. I vowed to go to school and get an education so I could work in corporate America. I was overtaken with emotion, and tears filled my eyes at the thought of having the freedom that I had never had before. Yes, I was scared. America was a foreign place, and I didn't know anyone there. I did have family there; however, I didn't really know them because of age and geographical distance. I came to discover that they're some of the most lovely and generous people that I'm proud to call family.

When we reached the third camp, I was so relieved. It had taken a long time to get there. After three and a half years (1984 to 1987 ), we had to undergo many health examinations before we would be allowed to continue our travels. When we were in the third camp, we were pricked, probed, prodded, and sometimes humiliated in these examinations, but it was part of the price to pay for freedom. If we failed any of those tests, we had to stay and take medications until we were deemed safe for travel. Some people took those medications for years … some were never able to leave. I can only wonder about their fate.

I'm big on hope. I've discovered that people need hope to survive. When people were told they were not allowed to leave the camp, they lost hope. Sadly, many committed suicide. Almost every single day, someone would become so despondent that they would kill themselves, and sadly it was most often by hanging. Tragically, some of those people would have learned the very next day that their names were posted in the column "cured and available for release." I learned that when they lost hope, they clearly lost their freedom ... their life.

The health examination was a major hurdle. After two months at the third camp, we made the list and got the green light to leave. Our years-long journey was finally on its last leg. We were going to America.

We arrived in American at LAX with one cardboard box that contained all of our worldly belongings. We had no money or education and didn't know the English language. The America we had heard about was vastly different than we expected; in comparison to Southeast Asia where I had lived my whole life, it was like night and day. When I "got off the boat" in America, I remember being blown away by the mountains, traffic lights, manicured lawns and refrigerators. These things were surreal to me, yet my overwhelming sensation was that of sadness because I was feeling alone—very, very alone. But I was determined—determined to never again go hungry, to be in control of my life and never again to have experience the tragedies and horrors I'd witnessed under communism and in the refugee camp.

We had gone from a refugee camp surrounded by barbed wire … and there we were, setting foot on American soil. We were totally out of place. In addition to the feelings above, America was foreign, including the food, the scenery, the culture and customs. The images I had previously seen didn't exactly match the experience I was having.

For instance, some mountains had no trees—they consisted entirely of rock. I call them bald mountains, and to this day, their lack of greenery and trees still saddens me.

Then there was the food. Keep in mind that we had existed almost entirely on rice. The first time I tasted yogurt I was appalled. Yuck! I couldn't believe that people in America ate spoiled food. Thinking it had gone bad, I threw it away, something I've never done, and got another one. It was just as terrible. Certain that it was spoiled and rotten, I wondered if that was how it was in America. Even though the country was very rich and healthy, it was apparent that people actually ate spoiled, rotten food. I was confused.

At first, the cultural differences were shocking. Everything I had learned in my former culture didn't apply in the States.

In Cambodia, it was inappropriate for females to chat with men, especially if they were single. To do so was considered flirting, which was taboo. Another inappropriate behavior was looking at people in the eye, which was considered to be rude. We were taught that physical contact of any sort was unacceptable, so in our culture, there was no hugging or even shaking hands.

Then we entered America, where the norms were totally opposite. For many years, I found it difficult to carry on a conversation with other people. Not only did they look me in the eye … and expect me to do the same … but as an introvert, I felt intimidated and uncomfortable when speaking with others. In Cambodia, women were not encouraged to talk, so it was difficult for me to let go of my former expectations and adapt to this culture where people talk all of the time. It put me in an awkward position, because my quiet demeanor that was once highly appropriate now made me an outcast.

When I grew up, I was taught to obey and respect elders. This is one thing that I cannot let go of, and I hold that value very dearly. I've had to juggle many of my former teachings and expectations, balancing them delicately with the cultural norms and expectations in America. In doing so, I've tried to find a happy medium, one where I don't feel I'm violating the beloved customs of my former country but still have the freedom to express myself as I interact with others.

Clothes were a different story. Ours were so outdated and out of place that they looked like Halloween costumes on the streets of America. It was like we'd taken the Star Trek Enterprise and landed in the United States, almost like it was a different planet, instead of being just a different country.

The culture shock continued for years as I learned that words actually have more than one meaning. Take for example the word "screwdriver." I knew that a screwdriver was a long slim tool, but imagine my surprise one day at a friend's house when I was asked if I wanted a screwdriver. What? Who? Me?

"No, thank you," I answered, wondering why she would ask me such a question. I looked at the sink, thinking it wasn't clogged. Besides that her husband was a plumber, so I couldn't figure out why she would ask me if I wanted a screwdriver—he could have fixed anything that needed repair.

I looked under the sink to see if there was a problem, but nothing looked out of place. As my eyes roamed over the countertops, I noticed a blender, a gallon of orange juice, and a couple bottles of vodka.

*Hmm, I wonder if that might have something to do with it.*

Another friend walked in and my friend repeated the question. "Do you want a screwdriver?"

"Yes!" she said. Suddenly, she had my undivided attention. I watched her walk into the kitchen and proceed to pour the juice and Vodka together. Ahhh, I get it, I thought and started laughing. It really was quite funny.

If someone would ask me today if I want a screwdriver, I learned enough of the culture to say "Yes, but make it a virgin, please."

I'm still learning, and the process has been interesting and amazing. I'm no longer intimidated; today, I am excited to discover and learn more about the cultures and norms practiced in America.

Rather than feeling out of place, I have grown accustomed to being raised differently than Americans. I now feel fortunate to have experienced and lived in two very diverse cultures. They have each taught me valuable lessons and helped me to grow, evolve, and adapt. Seeing things from a different perspective has been quite enlightening, and as the years go by, the insecurity, self-doubt, confusion, and shock that I experienced upon arriving in this great country have been replaced with a broader understanding and respect, even during those times when I don't always agree with what I see or hear.

We're all different, even people from the same country. And we have so much that we can teach each other as we live and work together in this giant melting pot. Not one, but two countries have shaped me and shaped my heritage and values. For that, I am eternally grateful.

## Chapter Sixteen

### Going To School

When we arrived in America, I was aware that we had nothing, but yet I was happy. That might seem odd to some, since so many people base their happiness on their financial status, their house, their wardrobe, or their place in society. I knew we had none of those things, but I really was happy! Why? Well, we were blessed that we had arrived safely here, where we could finally experience the freedom that we'd never been afforded or privileged to know in Cambodia. One of those freedoms was more important to me than any other—the freedom and opportunity to go to school and finally receive a real education.

I was hungry, but I knew hunger and starvation well. It wasn't physical hunger that I suffered with, but the hunger for knowledge. I wanted nothing more than to go to school, and my brother felt the same. But I had a big obstacle—I didn't know the English language. If I wanted to go to school and get that education I so longed for, I had no choice but to learn the language.

During that time, I was sixteen years old, which placed me in the tenth grade of high school. They called me a sophomore, and it took me a while to understand what that meant. Oh, how I wanted to succeed and learn. I wanted to soak in everything that I was taught and be able to use it to succeed in this great country, but I felt that the language barrier was initially too great to overcome. I flunked tenth grade because of my poor ability to speak and understand the English language. It was difficult to learn, and even more difficult for me to adapt to the culture and overall environment. For some time, my accent was the source of my embarrassment, just as it became the object of ridicule by other students who rejected and criticized those who were different. They frequently chose to make fun of the way I pronounced words or inadvertently said something incorrectly.

There is so much to the English language. For those who speak it in their native tongue, they know nothing else, and, therefore, cannot understand the difficulties others may have in learning the many different ways to express a thought, a feeling, or even a word. Words can have more than one meaning. Words that sound alike can have more than spelling. Words that are spelled one way are pronounced in an entirely different manner, with silent consonants or vowels. And let's not forget slang, which is another language in and of itself. As a teenager, slang was commonly used among my peers, but I didn't understand so much of it. This, too, set me apart from other students, who would laugh at my haphazard attempts to verbalize myself, finding my English too broken, too stiff, or too limited for their approval.

But I persevered, refusing to give up. I eventually learned the language enough to successfully receive the gift of an education I so very much wanted. After graduating from high school, I took my education even further and went on to college, where I prepared myself for the opportunity to gain the skills and knowledge to pursue a career in my next destination—corporate America. Exactly ten years later to the month, I graduated and walked the graduation aisle at the Cal State University at Fullerton commencement ceremony.

This was not only my dream, but it was also the dream my parents wanted for their children from the day we were born. There is no doubt in my mind that I would not have been able to go to school if we'd stayed in Cambodia. My father had been right. America was where we needed to be. It didn't provide us with a better life—it provided us with the opportunity to create a better life. It gave us newfound freedoms, ones that we didn't take for granted, but instead, they were freedoms that we took advantage of, availing ourselves of an education that would give us the knowledge and skills we'd need to create a better life for ourselves and our families. I did not take this opportunity lightly, and I still don't.

So many people think of school as a chore. They avoid doing any more than necessary to get by, never realizing what their lives could be like without it. Mom always told us that an education is the greatest resource anyone can have. It is something I will use every day for the rest of my life. The more I know, the better my life will be. Perhaps, I am so adamant about receiving and valuing a formal education because it was once forbidden to me. Not only was it forbidden, but those who had an education were subject to rather severe punishment or even elimination. Under the Regime, teachers and educated professionals were considered a threat to the "Organization" because that form of rule could only thrive if people were ignorant to what was going on and how they could change it. Their philosophy that people who lacked an education were more vulnerable and would be dependent on the Angkar for survival was true. I didn't want to be dependent on anyone or any "system" for my survival. That's far too risky and limiting.

To me, the power and control over my own life, my future, and my status rests solely with me. The joy I felt in graduating from college was enormous. It almost felt like revenge against the oppressive anti-education culture of the oppressive Pol Pot and his regime. They were defeated; this little girl grew up to live in freedom, gain an education, and earn a professional salary. On top of that, you can only imagine my mother's elation at watching her youngest child, my brother Kosal, walk down that very same graduation aisle at the very same university that I walked. Mother's and Father's dream came true. Their values of education and freedom drove our actions and, despite all odds, all obstacles thrown before us, she prevailed; we prevailed. **Success is the greatest revenge!**

While school was not easy for me and there were hurdles to jump, nothing quelled my burning desire to learn. My mother instilled the values and, as it's been said, "when the values are clear, the decisions are easy." So I decided to get to the finish line of graduation, no matter what. I knew what it was like to have nothing, but with an education, I would always have something—something that could never be taken away or diminished. Homes and possessions are material things that can be taken away, and my parents faced that stark reality. Happiness, professional ability, and our position in society can always come and go—but the knowledge and education one receives can never go away.

There is an ancient Asian phrase that describes my philosophy well. "Dig the well before you are thirsty." Receive an education when it is available. Even if you don't know why you need to know something, learn it anyway. Once you have a well full of knowledge, you'll never be thirsty or hungry. You'll have the knowledge to support yourself and improve yourself throughout your life.

There is another saying, "Give a man a fish and he'll eat for a day. Teach a man to fish and he'll eat for a lifetime." Oh, how true that is, and it so aptly describes the differences between Cambodia and America. In Cambodia, they gave you a fish and you ate for a day. In reality, we got whatever the Angkar chose to give us, in whatever quantities they chose, but we had no way of feeding ourselves the next day or the day after that. In America, people have the gift of an education. They learn how to fish, how to support themselves, and with that knowledge, they will be able to find a way to eat each and every day of their lives.

So many take that for granted. I do not take it lightly. Because I know what it's like to be dependent on the government, I've starved. Because I now have a long-awaited education, my only hunger is for learning. My interest in learning and knowing has never waned and remains as strong today as it was when I anticipated going to school upon arriving in America.

Many years after graduation, while working in corporate America, I made it a point to continue to learn, to hone and improve my skills and knowledge. I found that it is beneficial, not embarrassing, to always be a student. There will never be a time in life when our thirst for knowledge should be satisfied. You don't have to sit in a classroom with a textbook open to continue to grow and learn. Learning is available everywhere, in many different contexts. Read books and soak in their lessons. Seek the best mentor and learn from him or her. Attend seminars and workshops and learn from others who are generously willing to share their knowledge. I excitedly grasp every opportunity to learn, and in doing so, I have learned one very important thing: The poorest person is not one who doesn't have money, but one who doesn't have a wealth of knowledge.

## Chapter Seventeen

### Walk A Mile In My Shoes

Not only did I go to school, but I also looked for a job as soon as I was old enough and able to get one. Like so many young teens, my very first job was at McDonald's. Not only did I gain some much needed experience, which I will talk about later, but I also received my very first opportunity to earn an income. In itself, that was empowering. Having my own money brought me a sense of freedom and pride. It also enhanced my sense of responsibility, knowing that the money I earned contributed toward my needs, while giving me the ability to ease the financial burden a little for my mother, an uneducated single mother trying to raise two children in a country that was new to her.

I remember one of my first and most important purchases. A pair of shoes. Not just any shoes, but sensible and comfortable shoes that I could wear to work and school. They weren't fancy shoes, chosen for being stylish or trendy. I didn't run out and buy cool flip flops or fancy high heels, for they would be frivolous. Instead, I bought reasonable tennis shoes, without swooshes or any other trendy logo. Now, I know that many teenagers have nice shoes, cool backpacks, and a fashionable wardrobe, but I didn't. Unlike those who have tennis shoes, casual shoes, and dress shoes—sometimes several pair of each in multiple colors and styles—I had just one pair of shoes, my brand new tennis shoes.

I wore those shoes every day for three years. Every single day. New shoes were a rarity in my life, and because of that and the fact that I had to work for them, I took very good care of them. I wanted them to last. Scratch that, I needed them to last. I never put them on or took them off without making sure they were properly tied and untied, and I cleaned them on a regular basis. I was aware that I was wearing the same pair of shoes day after day and year after year, but it didn't bother me. I accepted the reality of my situation. Money was scarce, and there were so many other areas where it was needed much more.

Of course, I felt somewhat embarrassed. I did want nice things, just like everyone else. But I was able to control that desire. I didn't want to make things any more difficult for my mother than they already were. I had learned long before that it wasn't appropriate to ask for or expect things that were beyond my means.

With that lesson, I learned how to control my spending so I would be able to afford the things I really needed, like an education. Because I didn't splurge on things that weren't necessary and saved my money whenever I could, I went through college without debt or the worries that debt creates.

Drop by drop, the bucket will fill up. That is as true of money as it is of debt. Little by little, everything adds up, creating more of the same. It doesn't matter if it's money or debt—it is equally capable of growing at the rate in which it's dropped into the bucket. Thankfully, my family's situation had embedded in me a desire to become financially independent, and I learned early on to avoid four-letter words like debt whenever possible.

During my years of schooling, I focused on studying, not trying to catch up to or keep up with my fellow students, attempting to fit in by accumulating a fashionable wardrobe and costly possessions. When I graduated and got a full-time job, and as time has gone on, I've continued to see people try to compete with others. They are trying to keep up with the Joneses and, as a result, sink deeper and deeper into debt. I still avoid letting that type of peer pressure affect my finances, preferring the peace of mind that comes from knowing I can live within my means and afford the lifestyle I've created for myself.

The lesson that I learned throughout life has taught me and carried me well throughout my life. By avoiding debt and the desire to have more in order to be more, I have been able to live without the stress of financial struggle. After I graduated from college, I could have bought 20 pair of shoes, but I didn't want to. I've learned that money is a precious commodity, one that shouldn't be thrown away and spent impulsively on things I don't really need. In reality, those things don't mean anything and the pleasure one receives from them is fleeting, only to be replaced in a short time by the desire for something different, bigger, or better.

My shoes served me well. They lasted for three full years. Those shoes got me through school and my first job.

When I applied for the job at McDonald's, the manager didn't want to hire me because I couldn't speak English very well at the time. The truth of the matter was, though, that I could understand so much more of the language than I could actually speak. But I was given a chance and got the job—one that didn't require me to interact or communicate with the customers. It was a janitorial job that involved sweeping and mopping the floor, wiping the tables and more.

That sounds pretty easy, right? Well, I thought so, too, until I actually tried it. Have you ever pushed a wet industrial-size mop? Believe me, it's heavy, especially when you have to push the big yellow bucket full of water along with it. At the time, I think I weighed a lot less than that mop and bucket. It was physical work and, at a busy place like McDonald's, it was a job that was never done. As soon as I finished cleaning and wiping, I'd have to do it all over again. To quote another Asian sage, "Wax on, wax off!"

As I was holding the mop, moving it across the floor, I recalled a pearl of wisdom my grandmother told me, back when I was very young. Grandmother said, "My little Neary, I love you so much. With your size, you'll never be able to earn a living by picking up and holding a big heavy pickax. You're better off learning how to make a living by picking up and holding a pen." She told me that I needed to work not by using my muscle, but my brain. I took that advice to heart. It is with 'grandmother's pen' that I have written these stories and share these insights with you.

She reminded me that the key to my treasure is going to be education, whether it's a formal education or not. Holding that pen was important. I listened to my grandmother. I thought she was right. Education is critical.

As mentioned earlier, my mom always respected education, and it is clear that she acquired that value from her mom, my grandma. While mom's education, is limited to street smarts, my dad was educated by the book in schools. We are both grateful for that because we all benefited from his perseverance toward education and his resulting career.

Our matriarch, Grandma, was completely right. Education is the key, particularly for a young girl of small stature. I was going to earn my living with my brain—the so-called "pen" that Grandma referred to. But until I had that education, I had to get any job I possibly could.

When I came to the United States, I knew I needed to get an entry-level job and I sensed that it needed to be at a company that believed in the value of training and education. For me, a brand new, off-the-boat immigrant, that company was McDonald's. Yes, the coveted Golden Arches! They really stress the importance of learning their tested and proven systems. In fact, before you buy a McDonald's franchise they insist that you attended their coveted 'Hamburger U.' That's right, a university built around a proven and successful franchise system—McDonald's. What better place for me than to start working at a company that was truly committed to training its employees. I applied and was accepted.

One day, I asked my manager at McDonald's if she could train me to work at the register because I knew I would do better doing mental work than physical work. She agreed to train me. Shortly thereafter, an employee who worked the register didn't show up to work, so, happily, I was given the chance to prove that I was capable of doing her job. From that instant, the manager recognized that I could do math and was easily able to make change without a problem. Also, I showed that I could accurately place orders and effectively communicate with customers. That was a turning point in my McDonald's career. After that, I was asked to work the register while someone else got to take over the dreaded job of pushing the massively heavy mop.

The cash register itself wasn't hard to learn. In fact, the process had been made as simple as possible. They really have their training systems down to a science. There were actually pictures of the food on the keys to assist us in quickly placing the orders. The register automatically input the amount of money and told us exactly how much change to give back to the customer. My manager noticed that I caught on fast and was able to zip through orders rather quickly.

Then one of the people who worked the drive-through called in that she was ill and unable to work. My manager pulled me off the register and instructed me to fill in for her at the drive-through window. This gave the manager an opportunity to see me capably handle another job function, so after that point, I worked both the front register and the drive-through.

I guess you could say I was the off-screen, real life version of the character in the movie, "Coming to America." By the way, that was actually the very first movie I viewed in the United States. The scene where the man boasted about how he started out with the job of lettuce cutter and so proudly was moved up through several positions was hilarious—until I realized I was doing the exact same thing! And, in reality, I could relate to his sense of pride because it actually felt really, really good.

Earning a wage at McDonald's was a good opportunity—but it certainly wasn't my lifetime plan. I didn't navigate thousands of miles, risking my life just to make an hourly wage. I knew I wanted more. However, working at McDonald's was a great opportunity to acclimate to this great nation. They taught me a lot. I learned much more than how to work a cash register, push a mop, and take orders. I learned to be a dependable, reliable, and responsible worker. Further, the experience reinforced my core belief to never, ever give up. I learned that I had to prove myself in order to show others that I can not only do a job, but that I could do it as well as or better than others.

I also learned that working at McDonald's, or any other place, is not beneath me. A job is a job, as long as it is an honest living. In my life, there were jobs that, at first, I wouldn't even consider until I let go of my ego, came back to my humility, and accepted my reality. Frankly, I'm grateful for each and every job that I've had thus far. Each was a blessing and has allowed me the opportunity to grow and improve. They've helped to guide me toward my passion and purpose, given me the opportunity to get the education I needed, as well as meet many people I would not have otherwise met. That's something considerably more valuable than just the income they provided.

As I drive across town or up and down the highways of this great country, I see opportunity everywhere. So many are blind to it, but it's visible to me, maybe because I once experienced a life where there was no opportunity, no growth, and no education. I feel a deep responsibility to use that opportunity, not only to better myself, but to make a positive influence in the lives of others. I didn't want to change the world, but I wanted to know that I made it a better place. I have the opportunity to do that now, and it's one that I don't want to let fall by the wayside.

Back when I was in Cambodia, during the Khmer Rouge Regime, I told myself that if I ever wanted a better life, it would be up to me. I watched as horrific punishments were imposed on fellow Cambodians, and at a very young age watched my father die a long and painful death. Memories of unending hunger will continue to plague me, as will the many other immoral conditions that resulted from the control of an uncompassionate and "Organization" that ruled with fear and pain. I fled my country and the only life I'd ever known to become a refugee, which was not only risky and dangerous, but it also was a continuation of dependency that broke the spirit of so many. Then I embarked on a different journey, one that filled me with both fear and promise. It was the journey toward the American dream that is freedom.

In Cambodia, America was known as the land of opportunity—a country where people could prosper, receive an education, and be free to pursue a better life. One only needs courage, commitment, and discipline to turn that opportunity into reality. It would have been easy for me to believe that I'd never get a job in America, not with my English skills (or lack thereof), but I refused to believe or accept that. I went out on a limb and tried, anyway. Then, I refused to accept the fact that I had to stay at the bottom of the proverbial ladder. Yes, I had gratitude and humility, but I also had a desire to do more and be more. All I had to do was overcome my self-doubt with positive talk and thoughts, then I had to believe in myself enough to speak up and ask for more responsibility.

My journey will not be for naught. The opportunity to prosper in a free world that was my father's dying wish will not be taken for granted. I fully intend to seize it and use it to make the world a better place—one where I can fulfill my life purpose. For I believe that all of my experiences molded me and taught me lessons that I would have never learned in other ways. It is those lessons that I apply every day in my quest to be the best I can be.

Oh, these feet have been barefoot. They've worn the same pair of tennis shoes every single day for three years. These feet have crossed rice fields and swollen creeks; they've tiptoed past aggressive dogs and fled soldiers. They've walked the same path time and time again to receive my daily ration of food and work in fields. They've crossed the border from Cambodia into

Thailand, and then crossed the world and stepped off a plane onto American soil for the very first time. Today, they stand firmly in a land of opportunity, instead of a land of oppression. There were times when the next step seemed too difficult, too challenging, but I told myself over and over again, "You can do it, Neary. Yes, you can."

Through it all, I've learned that I am a survivor. I am strong and capable of overcoming almost anything that is thrown my way, as long as I stop, breathe, center myself, inventory my assets, and take action. When I do, I realize that everything I need is already here—it is my responsibility to figure out what to do with it.

Freedom comes with responsibility. At one time, I had no idea what freedom looked like, but now that I do, I embrace it with the respect and gratitude it so very much deserves. It's a concept that cannot be fully appreciated until one no longer has it. When I was a child back in the refugee camps, I dreamed about the Statue of Liberty and her iconic torch, which to me was a beacon of light and hope that represented freedom and everything it stands for. But that freedom comes at a price. Generations of soldiers fought for it and protect it to this very day. In return for that freedom and opportunity, I believe we have a deep and profound responsibility.

During the Regime, Cambodians did everything they could to survive—to simply exist. But in America, we are availed the opportunity to *live* and create a life with meaning and purpose—one where we can use our gifts, our knowledge, and our freedom to make the world a better place. In the classic book, *Man's Search for Meaning,* Viktor Frankl states that man is self-determining, meaning that it is up to each individual to determine if they will give in to conditions or, alternatively, stand up to them. He equates freedom with responsibility. Stating that the two cannot be separated—that freedom cannot exist without responsibility—he recommends that the Statue of Liberty be balanced with a Statue of Responsibility that represents serving others and making the world a better place. I wholeheartedly agree. In fact, I've been in contact with a group that has been inspired by Dr. Frankl's proposal and is working on that Statue of Responsibility at the time of this writing. Freedom and Responsibility will stand tall as symbols of inspiration to millions. How wonderful.

At one time in my life, I lived in deplorable and inhumane conditions. I've witnessed the devastation to the body, mind, and spirit of an entire country when it is stripped of its freedoms. I don't regret any part of my life—I also don't believe my life was created by accident, but rather by design. Ultimately, it gave me unique insights, experiences, and lessons that I use every day. Today, it is my responsibility to stand up to those conditions and do everything in my ability to share the plight and circumstances of those who are not as fortunate and who are not afforded opportunities. It is a great responsibility, but one I humbly and gladly accept.

So often there is a choice. Literally, there are people who are dying, yet they are at peace and happy. They are blessed and grateful for every breath that they take. Others their bodies are healthy and have all the money and everything in the world they could want, except they don't have happiness. Why is that so?

In this book, the stories and life lessons I've shared assisted me in reaching a level of success and happiness that I have desired. It was my intention to pen this book so you, too, can benefit from those lessons and tools, and enjoy, claim, or reclaim that peace of mind that sometimes feel so darned elusive. Peace, purpose, and prosperity are your birthright, and even if it seems like the road you're walking is too tough and you can't go any further, take it from me, you can. If I could get from internment to fulfillment, I know that you can get there from your starting point.

Seems a bit daunting?

Why not S.B.C.I. and take massive A.?

## ACKNOWLEDGEMENT

There are so many extraordinary people and, of course, the Divine above, that I'm honored and grateful to come in contact with—both directly and indirectly.

I offer gratitude to the Divine above for sending to me a wonderful family, friends, and mentors. Thank you also for sending some of the 'other' not so nice beings, too. Without them, I wouldn't have recognized the differences between the two. All have been sent as a gift for my growth and development.

Thanks for sending people who have trust, faith, and confidence in me.

I have deep gratitude for my family—we began a long journey together and still have many celebrations ahead of us. We stuck together through so much, shared plain rice with salt during our difficult times, and have celebrated feasts during good times.

Mom, you are my Angel sent from above. You are wise and brave. You are street smart, clever, and have more common sense than most. You've taught us the true and highest meaning of love, life, and compassion and that there's lots more to life than what appears on the surface. You are a special woman whom many kids in this world would love to have as their mother. Without you, my Angel, we would not be who and where we are today. You keep on reminding us always to have compassion and respect for all human beings and life forms. You invoked our good ethic and constantly reminded us to never forget who I am and who we are as a family. You didn't have to do all you'd done, but you did because of your enormous love for us. Mom, you showed us the power of a mother who can and will act fearlessly, do and make the seemingly impossible become possible, and showed us the true love between a mother and her kids.

My father, one of the Angels looking and smiling at us from above, was a very wise, deep, and methodological thinker. Even on your deathbed, you picked up a tiny pencil, endured the pain and suffering to write an alphabet at a time for a few months to complete a letter on a piece of cement paper bag. It'd take a healthy person a few minutes to complete writing the letter to my half-brother.

You proved to us even on your deathbed that once you've had a solid education, no one can take it away from you.

To my little brother, Kosal—even though you're bigger and weigh more than me, you are still my little brother.

You were a good boy who has grown to be a great man. Our journey had been rough at times, very rough. However, you were always caring, loving, and compassionate. I love you then, now, and will always love you.

To my oldest half-brother, Vanny, and his wonderful family, thank you for respecting father's request to sponsor us. We were a world apart, but your heart remained connected to us. My family discovered the family that we only heard of is generous and full of compassion. We thank you and are grateful for your help in assisting us.

To David M. Corbin, an Angel, my trusted mentor, strategist, and entrepreneur. You've an incredible ability to listen and understand both at personal and business levels. You dissected and strategized the possible roadmap I've to take toward achieving my life purpose. You gave me the clarity that I needed. In addition, you're a visionary, witty and humorous. You inspire me to be more than I can be. Your heart is over-filled with love, compassion, and caring for all livings. I knew there is at least one great mentor on this earth who could understand and help make my dream become a reality. It took me a long time to find you. The searches were well worth it.

Patti McKenna, your dedication and kindness in helping and creating this book comes to live is paying it forward toward you and your family. I'm grateful for you.

Ronita Godsi, your attention to detail, effort and the "must do it right" and "on time" delivery attitude with a huge heart is very appreciative.

And finally, thank you, **gentle reader**, for reading this first book and sharing it with your family and friends. Even though the stories are mine, the lessons are ours. It is my intention that these lessons add values to you as you navigate **your own journey toward becoming the greatest, most amazing ... YOU**.

To you all, please know that your generosity, guidance, support, encouragement, friendship, insightful feedback of my manuscript, and hospitality have enlightened and taught me more than all my years of schooling and all the books I've read...combined.

**All lives are different and significant. We travel different roads to seek the same destination: Love, unity, compassion, freedom, happiness, healthy, peace of mind, humanity, wealth and much more.**

**Together, we can do what alone we cannot. Let's do this.**

## Wisdom That Smooths My Path

"Many can make millions, but none can make time." - Kosal Heng

"Times and conditions change so rapidly that we must keep our aim constantly focused on the future." - Walt Disney

"Be like a postage stamp. Stick to something until you get there." - Josh Billings

"Sometimes life hits you in the head with a brick. Don't lose faith." - Steve Jobs

"If you love life, don't waste time, for time is what life is made up of." - Bruce Lee

"Make bold choices and make mistakes. It's all those things that add up to the person you become." - Angelina Jolie

"If you want to awaken all of humanity, then awaken all of yourself." - Lao Tzu

"If you want to eliminate the suffering in the world, then eliminate all that is dark and negative in yourself." - Lao Tzu

"As we express our gratitude, we must never forget that the highest appreciation is not to utter words, but to live by them." - John F. Kennedy

"To keep the body in good health is a duty... otherwise we shall not be able to keep our mind strong and clear." - Buddha

"I've learned that people will forget what you said, people will forget what you did, but people will never forget how you made them feel." - Maya Angelou

"God grant me the serenity to accept the things I cannot change; courage to change the things I can; and wisdom to know the difference." - Buddha

"No one saves us but ourselves. No one can and no one may. We ourselves must walk the path." - Buddha

"The mind is everything. We become what we think." - Buddha

"Let there be smile on every face, Let there be Love in every heart, Let there be peace in every soul." - Unknown

"Not all of us can do great things. But we can do small things with great love." - Mother Teresa

"Sometimes the threat is not those that oppose you, it's those who were supposed to be beside you." - Anonymous

"Stay hungry, stay foolish." - Steve Jobs

"You must not lose faith in humanity. Humanity is an ocean; if a few drops of the ocean are dirty, the ocean does not become dirty." - Mahatma Gandhi.

"Holding on to anger is like grasping a hot coal with the intent of throwing it at someone else; you are the one who gets burned." - Gautama Buddha

"He who has a 'why' to live, can bear with almost any 'how'." - Friedrich Nietzsche

"Progress is a nice word. But change is its motivator. And change has its enemies." - Robert Kennedy

"There is one quality that one must possess to win, and that is definiteness of purpose, the knowledge of what one wants and a burning desire to possess it." - Napoleon Hill

"First they ignore you, then they laugh at you, then they fight you, then you win." - Mahatma Gandhi

"Believe in yourself. When you believe in yourself, there are many possibilities that open up for you." - Joe Sugarman

"There are no pleasures in a fight, but some of my fights have been a pleasure to win." - Muhammad Ali

"Don't stay in bed, unless you can make money in bed." - George Burns

"You don't have to be a genius or a visionary or even a college graduate to be successful. You just need a framework and a dream." - Michael Dell

"If you do not change direction, you may end up where you are heading." Lao Tzu

"The immature rice stalk stands erect, while the mature stalk, heavy with grain, bends over." - Cambodian Proverb

**References: Links were accessible at the time of publication**

*http://www.websitesrcg.com/border/camps/Khao-I-Dang-photos.html*

*http://en.wikipedia.org/wiki/Khao-I-Dang*

*https://www.cambodiadaily.com/news/old-photos-shed-new-light-on-refugee-camps-68306/*

*http://articles.latimes.com/1987-01-01/news/mn-1919_1_refugee-camps*

Biography: Pol Pot
*https://youtu.be/Bk_ezm5gVnc*

Killing Fields Refugees in Cambodia - Treating the survivors of the Khmer Rouge genocide
*https://youtu.be/Er7q_ZWNnAs?list=PL3O6CE6IMRpcPvsOyEL7SJwZCg_9k4kmh*

## About The Authors

**Neary Heng** immigrated to the US in 1987 from war torn Cambodia. After learning English, she became first in her lineage to achieve a college degree. She later applied her hard earned lessons discussed in this book to become a high achiever in corporate America for over 18 years. Witnessing job burnout and dissatisfaction, Neary left the corporate world to pursue her life purpose sharing her messages with the audiences, inspiring and empowering them to have hope and make their dreams come true, so that they could enjoy freedom and harmony moments.

**David M. Corbin** is a national best-selling author, award winning inventor and hall of fame keynote speaker. Know as the 'mentor to mentors', David has worked closely with business leaders, NY Times Best Selling authors, Cabinet Members as well as Solo-preneurs. His books have achieved number one status on numerous lists and are read worldwide.

## CONTACT

Please share your personal stories of success through S.B.C.I.A strategy.

Be sure to join our community by clicking on this link http://NearyHeng.com. There, you will want to share your stories and experiences in applying the SBCIA strategy. In doing so, you'll be inspiring so many others on their journey. Also, if you are still struggling in any way, you'll be able to discover how other members are successfully applying the SBCIA model to face their fears and challenges, what keeps them going and how they reached their objectives. Together, we will turn our own Internments into Fulfillment. Keep in touch.

**Neary Heng**
Website: _http://nearyheng.com_


No one accomplishes anything alone. No one! Over the last 30 years, I've teamed up and served as a consultant, mentor, colleague and advisor to hundreds of businesses - large and small. If you, or anyone you know, is interested in engaging a seasoned advisor, then I sincerely invite you to contact me directly at david@davidcorbin.com. I will be honored to see if there is application, value and fit. Together, we can accomplish so much.

**David M. Corbin**
Website: _http://davidcorbin.com_
E-Mail: _david@davividcorbin.com_

---

Made in the USA
Columbia, SC
13 September 2020

20299492R00089